Living Hope

Also by Philip Greenslade:

Published by CWR
Cover to Cover: God's Story, 2001
God's Questions, 2003
Leadership (revised edition), 2002
The Perfect Gift, 2002

In the *Cover to Cover Bible Discovery* series
Philippians: Rejoice! The King is Lord, 2003
Psalms: Songs for all Seasons, 2003
1 & 2 Thessalonians: The Coming that Completes the Story, 2004

Published by Paternoster
A Passion for God's Story, 2002

Cover to Cover Bible Discovery
1 PETER

Living Hope

PHILIP GREENSLADE

Copyright © CWR 2004

Published 2004 by CWR, Waverley Abbey House, Waverley Lane, Farnham, Surrey GU9 8EP.

The right of Philip Greenslade to be identified as the author of this work has been asserted by him in accordance with the Copyright, Designs and Patents Act 1988, sections 77 and 78.

See back of book for list of National Distributors.

The quote from *The Call* is reprinted by permission of Thomas Nelson Publishers from the book entitled *The Call*, copyright © 1998 by Os Guinness.

Unless otherwise indicated, all Scripture references are from the Holy Bible: New International Version (NIV), copyright © 1973, 1978, 1984 by the International Bible Society.

Concept development, editing, design and production by CWR.

Cover image: Stone

Printed in Finland by W. S. Bookwell.

ISBN 1-85345-322-6

Contents

Preface

First Peter has long been a favourite of mine. It was the first book of Scripture that, as a young preacher, I ever sought to expound during several months of Sundays to a kind and long-suffering congregation.

Peter is writing to social and spiritual 'exiles and aliens'. I agree with those who see the modern church in Western Europe, by analogy, as being 'in exile' – a marginalised minority in a secular, if not pagan, culture. This is no recipe for despair – not if we see the world through Peter's Easter eyes, and grasp the tough grace that enables us to be as different as God is different.

In all my current teaching ministry, and in the writing of this latest book in the Bible Discovery series, I am sustained by the encouragement of my wife Mary who 'reads' me as wisely as she does my scripts.

I am grateful to all who come hungry for God's Word on my courses at Waverley Abbey House, and to the brilliant team at CWR who have once more done a splendid job in editing, designing and producing this little book. I continue to enjoy the loyal and life-enriching friendship of Stuart Reid, Trevor Martin and Ian Stackhouse. I pay special tribute to my friend Sean Gubb who has done so much to facilitate my work at CWR over the years.

Despair is the most unoriginal sin and potentially the most destructive. It blights our outwardly cheery modern society in which a few succumb to self-harm, while many dull their ache, if not with drugs, then with excessive self-indulgence or all-consuming work.

But because of Easter, Christians are forbidden *not* to hope.

Ours is a deathless hope, even when it is an exercise of faith as 'hope against hope'. Relish then again with me the good reasons that Peter gives us for the living hope within us. I pray that as you do, 'the Spirit of glory and of God rests upon you'.

Philip Greenslade
Pentecost 2004

Four things worth knowing about 1 Peter

1 Peter was written by one of the original followers of Jesus

It has been said that in calling men to be His disciples, 'Christ ruined many careers'. Peter was no exception. Jesus changed his work from that of fishing for fish in the local lake to fishing for people in the ocean of the world's need. When he met Jesus, Peter lost his job but found his destiny.

Peter could say, 'I was there'; he was a 'witness of Christ's sufferings' (5:1; cf 2 Pet. 1:16–18). Peter knows what he's talking about. He writes about hope as if the memory of his betrayal and recommissioning by love are still fresh in his mind. He writes with mature wisdom, that old natural bravado tempered with humility, his faith refined in the furnace of failure. The first to confess Jesus as the Christ, the first to preach Him in the power of the Spirit, he is the first to acknowledge that it's all by grace. By grace Peter was the pebble who became a rock.

1 Peter was written from the capital city of the Roman empire

The letter which bears the apostle Peter's name and stamp was probably sent in or around AD 65 from Rome, as is indicated by the code name 'Babylon' (5:13). It was written with the help of Silas (or Silvanus), with greetings also from Mark, who is described as Peter's 'son', and from either an unnamed woman or, more likely, the church in Rome referred to as 'she'. It is possible that this circle of disciples at the heart of a 'Petrine' community in Rome is responsible for 1 Peter and that the letter contains the memories and message of their by now martyred leader. I have no difficulty, however, in seeing the apostle Peter as the immediate author of the letter, and this is the position that will be assumed in the discussion that follows.[1]

1 Peter is a powerful message of encouragement to groups of scattered Christians whom Peter may never have visited but who knew him by reputation.

These Christians lived in what has been called 'the backwoods of the empire' – in those areas of north-west Asia Minor bordering on the Black Sea (1:1). The order in which these areas are mentioned may suggest the route a messenger would have taken in delivering a letter to them.

1 Peter highlights the centrality of Jesus and His achievement

This letter enshrines for us some of the most crucial apostolic teaching on the Person and work of Jesus Christ. 'In your hearts set apart Christ as Lord' (3:15).

The plotline throughout the letter is the central place held by Jesus Christ in salvation and in the Church. Each section of practical instruction is linked to a powerful dogmatic statement about the

Person and work of Jesus. In this way Christian behaviour is firmly rooted in Christian truth; Christian ethics flows out of the fully Christian experience of salvation.

Key Christological statements occur throughout the letter, chiefly at 1:18–21; 2:6–8; 2:21–25; 3:18–22. They demonstrate that Jesus is crucial to the whole plan and experience of salvation and to our vision of discipleship.

1 Peter was written to Christians under pressure to conform to society

Peter's readers seem predominantly to be Gentiles (cf references to their pagan past in 1:14; 2:10–11; 4:3ff.; 4:15), with perhaps some mixed Gentile-Jewish congregations.

They are undergoing trials (1:6; 2:12; 2:19; 3:16; 4:12ff.) which, though painful, seem to fall short of full-scale official persecution. The hostility is verbal rather than physical (3:9; 3:16; 4:14).

At this point it may be worth saying that 'suffering' in the New Testament must never be confused with 'sickness'. The pressure is that of resisting conformity to a godless culture, the pain of social ostracism, the frustrating awkwardness of being different. We should never underestimate this, as Luke Johnson points out:

> Suffering is no less real, however, for its not leading to death. Persecution and martyrdom, after all, have a certain clarity and comfort. Lines of allegiance are obvious. However painful the choice, it need be made only once. But scorn and contempt are slow-working acids that corrode individual and communal identity. Social alienation is not a trivial form of suffering. Persecution may bring death, but with meaning. Societal scorn can threaten meaning itself, which is a more subtle form of death.[2]

This raises the classic and highly relevant issue of the

Christian's relation to the surrounding culture. How can we be *in* the world but not *of* it? How can Christians be the salt of the earth without losing their savour? Can we be definitely different from the world without becoming merely odd or eccentric?

This is the question confronting Christian living and evangelism in every age: How can we permeate the culture without being conformed to it?

First Peter touches on all these issues and more. Drawing on extensive Old Testament knowledge, echoing truths held in common with James and Paul, and especially recollecting the words of his master, Jesus, the apostle Peter gives us his powerful message of hope for tough times. We will hear the strength of this if, in the next section, we probe more deeply into *the social setting* of Peter's readership.

Accessing the 1 Peter website!

The 'aliens' have landed and have turned out to be us!

We can begin to visualise more clearly the social setting of Peter's readers by noting that he describes them as 'strangers' or 'exiles' (*parapidemmos*, 1:1).

The question arises: Is this a theological description or a sociological assessment?

Influential modern scholarship, led by J.H. Elliott, has argued that it is their *sociological condition* that is primarily in mind here. According to this analysis, Peter's words apply first of all to the social location of his Christian readers as among those socially marginalised people who were 'resident aliens' and 'temporary residents or sojourners' even before their conversion. From a legal point of view such people would have been landless, homeless and without inheritance prospects. With few rights, and having low status in the eyes of society, they would already be vulnerable to threats and discrimination.

The most recent evangelical commentator on the letter, Scot McKnight, in general accepts this view, believing that Elliott 'has proved his case beyond reasonable doubt and a significant number of scholars on 1 Peter agree with him'.[3] If the social meaning is basic to the readers' condition then, says McKnight, 'the group of churches … was composed almost entirely of persons drawn from the slave classes and the disenfranchised'.[4]

Others dissent from this growing consensus, arguing that the language of exile and estrangement refers only to the *spiritual condition* of those for whom, in the words of the old song, 'this world is not my home, I'm just a-passing through'. The NIV reading supports this view by adding to the notion of 'strangers' the phrase 'in the world'. By doing this it opts for the idea of Christians as pilgrims who are heavenbound and mere transients in the present age. At its best this point of view is not positing an escapist 'going to heaven when we die'. Rather, the journey begins at baptism in a commitment to following in the footsteps of Jesus that will eventually lead to a lasting inheritance and final salvation (1:4,9) but, along the way, creates a distinctive lifestyle. Pilgrims will always have a different set of values from those who have settled down.[5]

I doubt the need to pose these two positions as extremes between which we are forced to choose. Whether or not Peter's readers were socially disenfranchised *before* their conversion, there can be little doubt that embracing the gospel would have sharply exacerbated their sense of social strangeness. 'Attempting to improve their social lot through membership in the community which the Christian movement offered, they experienced instead only further social aggravation. Now they were demeaned not only as social strangers and aliens but as "Christ-lackeys" as well.'[6]

Becoming a Christian calls into question many of society's values, and new converts might well have experienced hostility and suspicion. This is as true today as it was then. Furthermore, 1 Peter sees the Church as God's eschatological people whose sights are set on the future glory that now determines the shape and direction of their lives.

Peter wants his readers to know that the grace of the gospel more than compensates for any loss of social status or current security. Fully aware of their predicament, Peter tells them that 'although they are indeed estranged from their society religiously now as well as socially, their salvation is assured'.[7]

Fellowship with the divine Trinity, to which the gospel introduces us, provides the 'homeless' with a new and permanent home. When God loves you and accepts you in Jesus Christ you gain a brand-new and distinctive identity. However socially marginalised, you gain a whole new status as one of the people who belong to God and share His honour and patronage. Churches made up for the most part of poor, hardworking converts, with perhaps a few richer and more influential members, find new life in Christ and with Him a new society with a new network of family relationships.

Scattered like seed

Exiles of the 'Dispersion' is how Peter views his readers. This, too, is best read at its basic level as a socio-geographical description. Peter echoes the classic Jewish depiction of God's people when distanced from the promised land as living in the 'Diaspora' – the scattering of God's people as seed throughout the pagan world.

Peter applies the language of the Diaspora to the far-flung communities of believers in Christ across Asia Minor. They need look to no 'Jerusalem' across the sea for the living Christ in their midst is their centre. They need hark after no pilgrimage to a distant Temple because they can come to Christ every day and be built into His spiritual house.

Unrecognised they may be in their own small social world, but they are the very seeds of the kingdom of God scattered for sowing and fruit-bearing across the whole Roman empire. In such circumstances they may appear not merely disconcertingly odd but dangerously subversive.

We do not need to overdraw our distinctiveness by deliberately being weird or gratuitously offensive. The last thing we need is for Christians to turn themselves into the kind of caricatures of the real thing that our critics relish. This has nothing to do with being quaint, old-fashioned, or socially inhibited, and everything to do with being faithful to the gospel.

If the aliens have landed and do indeed turn out to be us then our efforts at 'normality' may be self-defeating. For all our complacent compromising with the culture, we can't shake off our strangeness. For all our fearful attempts to assimilate to society and to blend in with our surroundings, we inevitably stand out as different. If our faith and life in Christ are in any way authentic then even our well-meaning attempts at being relevant cannot entirely blunt the Christlike angularity of our shape in the world. Whether we wish it or not, we remain members of God's awkward squad. As the great Christian writer, Flannery O'Connor, once quipped, 'You shall know the truth and the truth shall make you odd!'

An oft-quoted passage from the *Epistle to Diognetus*, which describes Christian life in the second century, is an early attempt to capture the paradox of believers being in the world but not of the world:

> Christians are not distinguished from the rest of mankind by country or by speech or by dress ... yet the condition of citizenship which they exhibit is wonderful and admittedly strange. They live in countries of their own but simply as sojourners ... they share the life of citizens, they endure the lot of foreigners, every foreign land is to them a fatherland and every fatherland a foreign land; they obey the established laws and in their own lives they surpass the laws ...

The Christian's 'court of reputation'

> The author of 1 Peter, sensitive to the fact that he writes to people whose self-respect has come under serious fire from without, dedicates the first two chapters of his epistle largely to affirming the honour that is theirs in Christ. [8]

What was the nature of the 'serious fire' which Peter's readers were coming under?

Early Christians in the Greco-Roman world proclaimed a message and embodied virtues that were at odds with the core values of society. So Christians were subjected to 'censure and other shaming techniques, designed to bring these deviant people back in line with the values and behaviours held dear by the surrounding culture'.[9]

Conversion cut off Christians from a great deal of social activity, much of which was buttressed by idolatry. If Christians became unpopular, it was as a direct consequence of their 'defection from the solidarity they formally showed with their pagan neighbours at public worship, at public festivals, at social gatherings'.[10]

The social distress felt by the churches which is causing Peter such pastoral concern may not have reached the stage of full-blown persecution, with lynching or executions. But it was painful, nonetheless, involving misrepresentation, slander, reproach, beatings and imprisonment. No doubt in some cases there was severe financial loss and economic hardship.

As David de Silva explains, 'The Jesus movement appeared to undermine the sacred and central values of the society, putting formerly good and reliable people into a subversive cult.'[11]

Social ostracism was the price paid for following Jesus so faithfully. At the very least, masters might become even more demanding of their servants, customers might boycott small craftspeople, and from there the pressure could intensify to more physical and official harassment.

Not surprisingly, the urgent pastoral aim of letters such as 1 Peter is to reassure readers of God's loving commitment to them. The focus of the believers is once more directed to the honour and glory bestowed by God as more than compensating for society's disapproval. Peter's aim is also to build up the Church as what David de Silva calls 'a court of reputation' which will itself reinforce the Christian virtues that set believers apart from the culture.[12]

But why was 'reputation' so important?

Honour and shame

I woke in a cold sweat from a bad dream in which – before a large congregation – I stepped up to the pulpit dressed only in pyjamas! Every preacher's nightmare, I guess. I felt confused, exposed, acutely embarrassed and humiliated. These are all reactions associated not with guilt – I had done nothing wrong – but with shame.

Peter's readers lived in what sociologists call an 'honour-shame society'. Social conventions were subtly nuanced to assess – like a barometer – who deserved respect and glory, and what was deemed valuable and precious. These are precisely the notes Peter strikes in his letter in seeking to firm up the true identity and status of his Christian readers.

Issues of honour still predominate in many societies today, as anyone reading this book in the Middle East or Asia will know. Even in Europe, especially within Latinised cultures, such matters matter. As philosopher and social commentator, Alain de Botton, notes, violence is the approved method of redressing supposed slights to the honour of one's family or tribe.[13] This is true for the Mafioso in Sicily and for the Caribbean drug gangs in inner-city London for whom showing 'no respect' can provoke savage revenge.

But these are only the most extreme ends of the social spectrum. Whereas, to oversimplify, the European culture which emerged from Christendom was *guilt* conscious, now it is increasingly *shame* aware. In a host of seemingly more benign ways, a preoccupation with honour and shame is now pervasive in Western culture, manifesting itself in what de Botton calls '*status-anxiety*'. This surfaces in the way modern people are fascinated with celebrity, set such store by financial or sporting success, and have an almost obsessive concern for self-image and identity.

In such a climate, as de Botton concedes, it may well only be Christians who can offer an alternative. In 1 Peter's terms, nobodies are somebodies not because they have made so much of themselves but because God has made something of them by grace. Society's adulation matters less because God has ennobled them as His special and royal people. Their sense of God-given value and identity is reinforced by the embrace of the Church, a non-competitive, accepting group which now acts as their 'court of reputation'. As de Botton says, 'In an ideal Christian community, the dread of what it will be like to live beside winners will be tempered and contained by a basic equality of dignity and resources. The dichotomy – to succeed or to fail and wither – will lose some of its excruciating sharpness.'[14]

This is the vision of 1 Peter. Honour, for the Christian, does not derive from society's approval or from one's social standing but from God Himself who is the Father and the Judge. It is God's scrutiny and verdict that counts (1:17; 4:5). God is the audience before whom we enact our lives. In the final reckoning, it is not notable acts of public service but the undergoing of 'various trials' in faithfully following Jesus that accrue 'praise, glory and honour' at the revelation of Jesus Christ (1:7).

This drastic reversal of fortunes and revision of estimates is directly connected to the vindication and exaltation of the shamed and crucified Jesus which lies at the heart of our faith. He suffered a degrading death as the Stone rejected by the expert builders of God's house, but was raised up by God and elevated by God's choice to be the One around whom His true temple is built (2:6a). Consequently none of those who throw in their lot with this Christ will ever be 'put to shame' (2:6b).

The ground of this confidence is the established work of salvation wrought by God in Christ. The blood of Jesus which was seemingly wasted in a humiliatingly sordid death is revalued by God as infinitely *precious* (1:19). The cross acquires redemptive worth as the 'payment price' or 'ransom' that sets us free.

So the Lord Jesus determines all that flows from His saving achievement. From Him and on Him and around Him, as the 'cornerstone' which is chosen and *precious*, is built God's spiritual house (2:6b).

In the world Christians face rejection and reproach, but '*honour* is for those who believe' (2:7). This alteration in a much-loved text probably more accurately reflects the Greek text and takes little away from it. It serves to indicate the movement in the text from Christ's own value to the way that we are valued in and by Him. This is exactly the point towards which Peter is moving in 2:8–10 as he highlights the contrasting destiny of believers and unbelievers.

The honour that accrues to us in Christ is the honour of participating in His vindication before God, and in never being put to shame but sharing in His as-yet unrevealed glory.

The challenge that confronts us now, as then, is to walk courageously in His footsteps even though suffering is the path to life (2:21ff.). Our 'falling into Him' in humble trust leads to our exaltation with Him (5:6).

David de Silva summarises well the cruciform shape of this reversal of values: 'Jesus' case becomes then the demonstration of the ignorance and upside-down mentality of the society, as well as the guarantee of the reversal and vindication that God will grant to all Jesus' followers.'[15]

The aim of Christians in society is not to undermine social order and cause upheaval for its own sake. We are not to be busybodies or self-serving social nuisances. We are to be real revolutionaries, lovingly and humbly bent on transforming society in ways which relativise the Roman ideals of honour and glory without despising them.

Peter's is shrewd counsel. In J. Ramsey Michaels' assessment, 'This brief tract written in a culture not yet Christian becomes a relevant textbook on Christian living in a culture that is no longer Christian.'[16]

Outline of 1 Peter

God's People are Different

1:1–2   Life in the eternal triangle

1:3–4   Living hope, lasting heritage

1:5–9   Gold-standard faith

1:10–13 Salvation in three tenses

God's People Dare to be as Different as God

1:14–16 Father's look-alike children

1:17   Fear that takes God seriously

1:18–21 Freedom from futility through the cross

God's People Live Differently Together

1:22–25 Purified by truth for love

2:1–3   Purified by grace for growth

2:4–8   Privileged with a threefold purpose

2:9–10   Privileged with a fourfold identity

God's People Behave Differently in the World

2:11–12 Living differently as strangers

2:13–17 Living differently as subjects

2:18–20 Living differently as servants

2:21–25 The cross makes all the difference
            redirects our steps
            revokes the law of retaliation
            removes the burden of sin
            renews our life
            restores our relationship with God

God's People Think Differently about the Good Life

3:1–7   Sharing the good life – as spouses

3:8–12   Sharing the secrets of the good life – as brothers and sisters

---

God's People React Differently to Pressure

3:13–14 Suffering bravely

3:15–17 Sanctifying Christ as Lord

GOD'S PEOPLE ARE DIFFERENT

1 PETER

1:1-2 Life in the eternal triangle

[1]Peter, an apostle of Jesus Christ,

To God's elect, strangers in the world, scattered throughout Pontus, Galatia, Cappadocia, Asia and Bithynia, [2]who have been chosen according to the foreknowledge of God the Father, through the sanctifying work of the Spirit, for obedience to Jesus Christ and sprinkling by his blood:

Grace and peace be yours in abundance.

'Peter, an apostle of Jesus Christ' – what a story that tells! A conventional enough letter opening but behind it lies a stirring history of grace. The pebble finally became the rock on whose confession of Christ the Church was built.

Peter writes to those he describes as 'God's elect, strangers … scattered throughout' what is now part of modern Turkey. The NIV rather tendentiously inserts the phrase 'in the world' which reads more crisply in the ESV as *'elect exiles of the dispersion'*. This reading helpfully preserves the reference to the 'Diaspora', the classic Jewish term for God's people exiled from the promised land and scattered as seed in the wider Gentile world.

In Richard Bauckham's view, the phrase 'exiles of the dispersion' is the 'controlling image which overarches everything 1 Peter has to say about its readers' identity and situation'. It serves, he suggests, 'as a potent theological interpretation of the facts of Gentile Christian existence'.[17]

Peter's readers may or may not have been already socially marginalised and disenfranchised but there is no doubt that God, through the gospel, has lifted them into a whole new realm of reality as members of His chosen people and that this has set them apart from their culture and traditions so that they think and behave differently.

They have been embraced by the Trinity love and life of the one

Creator God who had once chosen Abraham's descendants to bring blessing to the world and the people of Israel to spearhead His redemptive movement among the nations.

The writer sees these mostly Gentile converts, therefore, as in some sense continuous with the age-old purposes and people of God. Viewing them in this light, he has no qualms about applying to them language that is heavily laden with Old Testament and Israelite connotations. It is no surprise, then, to see the familiar Old Testament terminology of *election and exodus* permeating this opening section of the letter.

Particularly important to Peter is the way the prophets – in particular Isaiah in chapters 40 to 55 – envisage God's future act of salvation as a *new and greater exodus*. Peter is sure his readers have experienced for themselves that saving work of God which was always intended ultimately to reach Gentiles like themselves. So, like the prophets before him, he ransacks the terminology of the first exodus from Egypt to describe this experience.

We need to be careful here in adducing what Peter is, and is not, doing when he employs this Israel-specific language to ex-pagans. In doing this he is not implying that Israel's unique identity has simply been transferred to the Church, as if the Church replaces Israel. Nor is he merely making an analogy between that unique identity and the new status of Gentile converts.

Something more subtle and more profound is going on here. Peter – like the other apostles – is celebrating the *renewal and expansion* of God's people which was promised by the prophets. That newness and enlargement is now a reality in Jesus Christ for both Jews and Gentiles so that even those once regarded as 'not God's people' have become 'God's people' (2:10). If Peter seems to lay less emphasis on the continuity it is because he is relishing the radical new state of affairs which has come to both Jew and Gentile in Christ and, in particular, because he is keen to bolster the courage and sense of status of the Gentile Christians he is mainly addressing. His Gentile readers, he assures them, have not simply been grafted on to Israel's history as latecomers but, together with all Jewish Christian believers, are even now sharing in Israel's long-awaited future.

For this reason, 1 Peter – especially in its first two chapters – is soaked in the prophetic vision of Messianic salvation, as the actual citations of Isaiah indicate: 1 Pet. 1:18/Isa. 52:3; 1 Pet. 1:24–25/Isa.40:6–8; 1 Pet. 2:22/Isa.53:9; 1 Pet. 2:23/Isa.53:7; 1 Pet. 2:24/Isa.53:4–5,12; 1 Pet. 2:25/Isa.53:6; 40:11.

In particular, Isaiah 43:19–21 provides the parameters for 1 Peter's rich reminder of Christian identity and vocation:

> See, I am doing a new thing!
>> Now it springs up; do you not perceive it?
> I am making a way in the desert
>> and streams in the wasteland.
> The wild animals honour me,
>> the jackals and the owls,
> because I provide water in the desert
>> and streams in the wasteland,
> to give drink to my people, my chosen,
>> the people I formed for myself
>> that they may proclaim my praise.

With Isaiah 43:19–21 compare 1 Peter 1:2 and 2:9: 'chosen … that you may declare the praises of him who called you …'

The Church, then, is being described as the people God has created for Himself through the achievement of Jesus Christ, His Suffering Servant and Passover Lamb, who are called into being by His life-giving Word in the gospel.

In what sense are Christians still 'exiles in dispersion'? Three further considerations may be offered at this point:

- The exodus they enjoy is not a geographical one but a decisive spiritual movement, so the Egypt they have left behind and the

Babylon they must come out of is 'the empty way of life' inherited from their fathers (1:18).

- They are no longer cut off from a distant centre – the Temple in Jerusalem to be visited on pilgrimage perhaps once in a lifetime – but through the Holy Spirit and in Christ they themselves form a 'spiritual house' for worship right where they are (2:4ff.).
- The return from exile has truly began but will only be complete when believers enter into their future heavenly inheritance (1:4).

Richard Bauckham helpfully concludes that 'the new identity the readers are given as exiles of the Diaspora is one which interprets their experience of social alienation and hostility, and enables them to understand it in the context of an identity which transcends it'.[18]

1:2

If Peter's readers need reassurance in the light of their cultural isolation and insecurity, these words provide it! In the face of social exclusion they enjoy nothing less than full and extravagant inclusion in the Trinitarian life of the one Creator God.

Let's relish the details.

1) *Chosen by God the Father for relationship with Himself*

For Israel and for the early Christians the word 'chosen' contained none of the threat it seems to pose for many modern Christians. 'Chosenness' scares us moderns perhaps because our perception has been coloured by arid and ruthless philosophical discussions about predestination, and so we have developed an aversion to the concept. Furthermore, our inbuilt distaste for determinism of any kind has been exacerbated in the modern world by our hijacking of the notion of freedom to mean only one thing – self-determination.

In truth, God's freedom of choice is precisely what leads to our freedom (1:18). That God in His mercy chooses freedom *for us* frees us to make choices *for Him* (see 2:16).

As far as biblical believers are concerned, election is simply the language of love (cf Deut. 7:7). It is essentially language for 'insiders'. It is meant to reassure us that our place in God's family and heart does not finally depend on our merit or resolve but rests entirely on His loving initiative and ongoing grace.

God's choice of us has been made 'according to the foreknowledge of God the Father'. That is, He chose us in full awareness of all that might be known about us, including the precariousness of our present social condition and all-too-human propensity for future failure and defeat. Knowing all this, He sets His love upon His people. Think of yourself, then, as handpicked, and be strengthened in your identity and self-worth.

2) *Consecrated to this relationship by means of the Holy Spirit's 'sanctifying work'*

Here, too, Peter employs the richly textured holiness language of Israel's tradition. The primary reference is to the activity of the Holy Spirit *in conversion*. This may come as a surprise to those of us within the evangelical tradition for whom such language usually applies to post-conversion progress in transformed living. Evangelicals, wary of supposed Catholic confusion on this matter and fearful of allowing good works to intrude on the pure grace of salvation, have often split justification and sanctification. But this is not borne out by the New Testament writers who can, on occasions, speak without embarrassment of conversion as an act of sanctification (eg 2 Thess. 2:13; Heb.10:10).

Sanctification or consecration may be viewed as three stages:

- initial separation from sin and idolatry unto God at conversion (cf 1 Cor. 6:11),
- continuous growth in holy living (eg 1 Thess. 4:3),

- the final action of God when He makes us complete (Eph. 5:26–27).

Here in 1 Peter 1:2 the emphasis is on the *initial* stage, when the Holy Spirit breaks into our lives and makes us God's own people and possession. In this way we are set apart *to* God and *for* God. That is, we are reserved for God's glory and to do God's will. The ongoing work of the Holy Spirit, then, maintains us in this sphere of spiritual reality so that everything we do is sanctified to God's service.

By His action, also, we are set apart *from* the world *for* the world! Our consecration to God entails being set apart *from* the world so that we no longer walk in futile ways as the pagans do (1:18; 2:11; 4:3–4). Christian virtues and practice are no longer determined by inherited ideas or social fashions but by the gospel.[19] But if we are set apart *from* the world it is *for the sake of the world!*

No one in recent times has more faithfully urged this vision on the Church than Stanley Hauerwas. He writes characteristically:

> The first social task of the church – the people capable of remembering and telling the story of God we find in Jesus – is to be the church and thus help the world understand itself as the world. The world, to be sure, is God's world, God's good creation, which is all the more distorted by sin because it still is bounded by God's goodness. For the church to be the church, therefore, is not anti-world, but rather an attempt to show what the world is meant to be as God's good creation.[20]

3) *Cleansed by the blood of Jesus*
The language of 'sprinkling' immediately and vividly recalls the Jewish sacrificial system. In particular, it echoes Numbers 19 where the blood of a red heifer is applied to the tent of meeting, and its ashes, after burning, are mixed with water and sprinkled on

those attending the tent.

This purification is aimed – as is every facet of the Torah – at maintaining covenant relationship. Peter's words also draw on the narrative of the sprinkled blood of the sacrificial animal which ratified the covenant at Sinai (Exod. 24:3-8). It is the blood of Jesus which inaugurates the new covenant realities enjoyed by Christians (cf Mark 14:24; Heb. 9:18–21; 10:22; 12:24). The only ground of our being God's consecrated people is the 'blood applied to us' as the Holy Spirit seals us in a new covenant relationship with God.

Jesus is our Shepherd;
For the sheep He bled;
Every lamb is sprinkled
With the blood He shed;
Then on each He setteth
His own secret sign;
'They that have My Spirit,
These', saith He, 'are mine'.

Hugh Howell

So our lives are:

4) *Claimed by God for Christian discipleship*
'Obedience to Jesus Christ' refers here first to the initial surrender of faith that embraces the gospel and confesses Jesus as Lord in conversion (cf 1:22; Rom. 1:5; 15:18; 16:26). Beyond this our conversion commits us to a lifelong journey of following in the footsteps of our Lord and Master Jesus Christ (eg 2:21ff.). He ventures all His trust in doing the Father's will (2:23) and models true sonship for us (1:14).

Again we may note how counter-cultural is any talk of 'obedience' or 'lordship'! The mainspring of our motivation is no longer an egocentric quest for self-fulfilment but a heartfelt reverence for the majestic Lordship of Jesus to which we gladly bend our minds and wills and which, in the end, offers the only rationale for our distinctive behaviour and reactions (3:15).

What a greeting all this is! Here is 'grace and peace' in 'abundance'.

Marginalised, vulnerable groups of Christians who live on the edge of society are assured of being at the centre of the Father's heart and plan. 'Homeless exiles' truly have a home inside the love-in-relationship which is God-in-Trinity.

Not surprisingly there is much to praise God for!

1:3–4 Living hope, lasting heritage

> ³Praise be to the God and Father of our Lord Jesus Christ! In his great mercy he has given us new birth into a living hope through the resurrection of Jesus Christ from the dead, ⁴and into an inheritance that can never perish, spoil or fade – kept in heaven for you …

These verses are part of one long sentence in the Greek which continues until the end of verse 12. Here is a great torrent of thanksgiving with each thought spilling over exuberantly into the next.

'Blessed be …' may be preferred to 'praise be …' if only because it preserves for us something of the flavour of the classic Jewish prayer style in which Peter shapes his praise.

The traditional synagogue prayer began just this way as a *berakah* prayer which offered a litany of 'blessings' to God. Such a genre of prayer reminds us always that we bless God only because He has first blessed us. Since the Greek verb Peter uses here is *eulogeo*, we may describe this section as one long 'eulogy' to the Father.

The first great reason for praise is that God's mercy has given us new birth into a *living hope*. 'Mercy' is the manifestation in a human story conditioned by sin and ripe for pardon of God's own unchanging disposition to show His face as gracious and compassionate (cf Exod. 34:6). This is our God, abounding in love and faithfulness, who drags His feet to show anger and leaps to loose the sinner's chains. This is not extrinsic to God's own nature but, as verse 2 asserts, an overflow of His Trinitarian life. In Colin Gunton's words, 'Mercy is the outworking in a fallen time and history of the action of God for whom love of the other is central to his being'.[21] On such a God all our hope is founded.

Human valuation may have written us off as hopeless cases but God's infinite mercy has given us a 'living hope'! This connects to the startling reversal of human verdicts and valuations that lies at the heart of our gospel (see again 2:4ff.).

If the memories of the apostle Peter do in any way lie behind this letter then he could provide irrefutable testimony to the mercy of God. Peter had been there. In the bitter aftermath of his betrayal what hope of recovery could he possibly entertain? Meant to be the rock, he had crumbled into the dust of disloyalty. But Jesus had prayed for him and he had turned again, now fitted to be the wounded healer of the brethren. He had scurried off in shame to the comfort zone of fishing that he knew best, only for relentless love to seek him out and win him over and give him a second chance. Peter no doubt could be the patron saint of lost causes, the alchemist of grace and rekindler of burnt-out dreams.

Our lives, we know only too well, hang on hope. Hope deferred, said Israel's sages, makes the heart sick. Hope is the headlights on the dark road ahead. You cannot drive without it.[22] 'Hope is the oxygen of the soul'; when it dies, something precious curls up and dies inside us.

Thanks to modern science we no longer believe we live on a flat earth. But the price has been a flattened heaven. All we seem left is hedonism of a grimly materialistic and sensual bent or bored despair. Hopelessness is living under a low-roofed, one-dimensional world whose ceiling is painted sky only feet above our head. Living hope, on the other hand, says Peter Kreeft, 'gives us height, and room. It puts us outdoors, outside this stuffy little idol called society, in a cosmos that sprouts turrets and spires.'[23]

Such true transcendence lifts up our hearts and inspires us to 'lift up our heads for the redemption that draws near'. For such hope there is no substitute.

The counterfeiters try. False hopes are ten-a-penny. From Charles Dicken's Mr Micawber, whose perennial mantra was that 'something will turn up', to the last-ditch gamble that 'where there's life there's hope', we clutch at straws to keep hope alive. In our modern world the inflated claims made by advertisers for their products and the propaganda and spin of politicians and powerbrokers combine to make us suspicious of any prospect of 'fine weather' ahead. It takes the gospel to enable us to tell the difference between *hope* and *hype*.

Living hope, then, may be highlighted as the master theme of the whole thanksgiving which anticipates the reminder that through Christ our 'faith and hope are in God' (1:21). Through the gospel 'hope springs eternal'.

Peter celebrates his reasons for the hope that is in him (cf 3:15). The first source of hope is *regeneration* (1:3).

Relish the miracle of 'new birth' on which hope relies.

'Can a leopard change his spots?' asked the prophet (Jer. 13:23). Can human nature be changed? 'She'll never change' is a sentence of psychological doom. Mysterious as it is, we can be changed by 'new birth' – by the Holy Spirit (John 3:1ff.).

It is sad that the epithet 'born again' has become a tired cliché, trivialised and applied to anyone who claims to have prayed the 'sinner's prayer' some time somewhere. It is regrettable that within evangelism 'born again' has been routinised and reduced to four steps to take.

In his brilliantly written and spiritually bracing book, *Your God is Too Safe*, Mark Buchanan has powerfully inveighed against this tendency. He writes, 'It's an irony that Jesus' famous statement to

Nicodemus, you must be born again, has in our hands been turned into a slogan and a formula. Out of Jesus' mouth, in Nicodemus' ear, that statement proclaimed a staggering mystery. It was the ultimate anti-formula.' But, he goes on, 'This is a description of the inbreaking and surprising move of God. This is something we can't work for, work up, predict, direct. It doesn't slot neatly into a programme. You just hear it coming and fling yourself headlong into the hurricane.'[24]

That this is not some irrational leap in the dark or flight of mysticism is clear from what Peter goes on to say in 1:23: 'For you have been born again, not of perishable seed, but of imperishable, through the living and enduring word of God' – that is, through the Word preached to us as the gospel. As at the beginning, God's Spirit and God's Word combine to strikingly creative effect.

More of this later. For the moment we follow the sequence of Peter's words.

The mercy of God made known in the miracle of new birth derives its energy and meaning from the *resurrection* (1:3). This is further 'reason for the hope that is in us'. 'Living hope' arises directly out of the resurrection of Jesus.

The two disciples trudging home to Emmaus, disconsolate like all the other followers of Jesus after His crucifixion, spoke of the promised future only in the past tense: 'we *had* hoped ...' (Luke 24:21). We had hoped that He was the One, the Messiah, the long-awaited deliverer. For a while a door seemed to swing open on God's salvation and kingdom, only to be slammed shut by His shameful death on the cross. In the tomb of Jesus, as in every cemetery, hopes decay and dreams lie buried.

What changed this? In a word, Christ's resurrection! He has broken through death, robbed us of our pitiable despair, and brought our hopes alive with Him (cf 1 Cor. 15:17–20). As Clement of Alexandria, one of the Early Church Fathers, said, 'He has turned all my sunsets into sunrise.'

Our hope is anchored in the past but it is not the dead past. We hope because of what has already happened within our history in the resurrection of Jesus which is a down payment of the all-transforming eschatological future awaiting us at the end of the story. Jesus Christ has been 'revealed in these last times'. However near or far from the end of the world as we know it, we surely live in the 'last days'. The ultimate and final reality of God's glorious future has already burst upon our jaded world. Through Him, crucified and risen, 'you believe in God, who raised him from the dead and glorified him, so that your faith and *hope* are in God' (1:21).

1:4

Children reborn in this way by God's resurrection Spirit and imperishable seed receive the guarantee of an 'inheritance' which lies beyond the reach of change and decay (1:4). The land of Canaan once promised to Abraham and his descendants turns out to be a microcosm of a much greater and more transcendent reality.

The ultimate inheritance of God's people is of the same lasting quality as those born to it.

- it, too, is *imperishable,*
- it is *undefiled* and unspoilt by the ravages of time,
- it is *unfading* – remaining as lustrous and radiant as the crowns it offers (5:4).

We would be mistaken to read this as a promise of something nebulous or ethereal of the pie-in-the-sky-when-we-die variety. The hoped-for inheritance is kept *in* heaven but is *not* heaven.

Our hope needs to be earthed by the prophetic realism of the Bible. Lewis Smedes, in typical fashion, comments:

When I do, which is rarely, itch for heaven I find that what I really want there is the fulfilment of all that is good about life now – but with its beauty never blotched with ugliness, its pleasure never choked with pain, its plenty never mocked by unfairness to others, its truth never hid by falsehood, its goodness never compromised by evil – and the discovery every day anew that our very beings are alive with God. In short, total fulfilment. Which is, I suppose, what we want when we want heaven.[25]

Of this we can be sure.

As if to leave no room for doubt, Peter assures his readers that their inheritance is being *kept for them* in heaven's safe-keeping and – to dispel any vestige of uncertainty – they, as heirs, are being *kept for it*, guarded by God's power until such time as it is revealed (1:4–5).

You don't have to be at a Billy Graham campaign to share Fanny Crosby's confidence:

Blessed assurance, Jesus is mine,
O what a foretaste of glory divine!
Heir of salvation, purchase of God;
Born of His Spirit, washed in His blood.

1:5–9 Gold-standard faith

[5]who through faith are shielded by God's power until the coming of the salvation that is ready to be revealed in the last time. [6]In this you greatly rejoice, though now for a little while you may have had to suffer grief in all kinds of trials. [7]These have come so that your faith – of greater worth than gold, which perishes even though refined by fire – may be proved genuine and may result in praise, glory and honour when Jesus Christ is revealed. [8]Though you have not seen him, you love him; and even though you do not see him now, you believe in him and are filled with an inexpressible and glorious joy, [9]for you are receiving the goal of your faith, the salvation of your souls.

All that Peter has celebrated so far of the new birth into a living hope which guarantees a future inheritance comes to us *'through faith ...'* (1:5). This 'throughness' of faith reminds us that faith is not a source but a channel by which we receive God's gifts.

Faith is a welcoming openness to God's moves towards us, not the forcing of a claim upon Him.

Faith is not 'faith in faith' as a power we possess. True faith is not a force but an act of trust in a trustworthy person, faith 'in' God (1:21).

Peter speaks first of faith being *refined* (1:6–7). This is the purpose hidden with the 'trials' we undergo as Christian believers.

In this context 'trials' become the tests by which we know if our faith can take the strain. God never tempts us to sin (James 1:13ff.), but He may allow temptation to cross our path, as He did with Jesus, to test how strong is our commitment and how firm our trust. Followers of Jesus should not be surprised by this (4:12). After all, Jesus had warned the original band of disciples that trials were to be expected as normal (John 16:33).

Trials, then, are faith's quality control. They serve to measure the genuineness of our faith. Peter's imagery is that of metals being proved (*dokimazo*) in a furnace. Faith which passes through such tests is shown to be precious and, as we might say, 'worth its weight in gold'.

Jesus had once used a different metaphor but the reality for Peter was the same. His faith had been severely 'sifted' but was miraculously preserved from complete collapse by the prayers of Jesus (Luke 22:31–32).

If the quietly confident tone of this letter is anything to go by, Peter's faith had long since been purged of its initial bravado. From his own personal experience, Peter urges us to see that trials can refine our trust and produce a 'gold-standard' faith that will, he assures us, meet with God's approval at the return of Jesus (1:7c). And because we may know the grace of finding meaning in our trials they may even become a cause for joy (1:6; cf James 1:2–3).

So he speaks of faith *rejoicing* (1:8). At this point Peter strikes a lyrical, almost mystical note. It is as if he himself, while dictating to Silas, is momentarily lost in wonder, love and praise.

Faith rejoices even in what is unseen. Peter would surely have agreed with the writer to the Hebrews that faith rejoices in the confidence of what is hoped for and the certainty of what is not seen (Heb. 11:1).

Genuine faith, tested by trials, finds its deepest joy not in getting things from the Lord but in deepening a relationship with Him. Faith's highest pleasure is in experiencing this close personal relationship of love with Jesus. Faith is an extension of love; love an enriching and strengthening of faith.

I sang as a child:

I think when I read that sweet story of old,
When Jesus was here among men,
How He called little children, as lambs to His fold,
I should like to have been with them then.

Who would want to disparage such a sentiment, but it is probably an unbiblical aspiration.

John records Jesus as saying to Thomas, 'Because you have seen me, you have believed; blessed are those who have not seen and yet have believed' (John 20:29). Uniquely foundational as his time with Jesus was (1 John 1:1-4), John wrote his whole Gospel to reassure his readers that they were not in the end put at a disadvantage by Jesus' departure (cf John 16:7). Contrary to expectation, then and now, *believing is seeing.*

What is clear, as A.W. Tozer noted, is that 'it is possible to love someone we have never seen, but it is totally impossible for us to love someone we have not "experienced" in some way'.[26]

When Helen Keller was taken to hear Caruso, she was allowed to place her fingers on his chest while the great Italian tenor performed a favourite operatic aria. She stood, it was said, transfixed as Caruso 'sang' to her through the reverberations she felt in her fingertips.

Peter's relationship with Jesus had been face to face but his readers by faith can enjoy it heart to heart. As J.H. Jowett once put it, 'Theirs was not the love born of gazing upon Christ's face, but the love begotten by communion with Him.'

Believing with passion begets intense and unutterable joy – a joy that is radiant with glimpses of what glory will be like! Again, the old hymns may best express devotion to the Jesus 'whose radiant form these eyes have never seen':

> Yet, though I have not seen, and still
> Must rest in faith alone,
> I love Thee, dearest Lord, and will,
> Unseen, but not unknown.[27]

When my wife and I visited our friend Vera on her one-hundredth birthday we found her sparkling with joy! She had dreamt, she told us with all the naïve enthusiasm of a young girl, of a door opening onto a beautiful garden. Beyond it stood Jesus who smiled, called her name and invited her to come through. 'I can't wait,' she said to us. 'I love Him so much I just want to throw my arms right round Him and tell Him how wonderful He is!' For her, and for us, sitting with her in the monastic stillness of the sheltered accommodation, her testimony felt as real as that of any of the noble saints and mystics fêted by Church history.

Has any historical figure inspired more faith than Jesus Christ? Has anyone been more loved? Has any other figure evoked such a depth of reflection and meditation?

I have just been reading Larry Hurtado's large and sweeping survey of the adoration of Jesus in the Early Church. In his introduction Hurtado noted:

Devotion to Jesus was exhibited in a unparalleled intensity and diversity of expression, for which there is no true analogy in the religious environment of the time. There is simply no precedent or parallel for the level of energy invested by early Christians in expressing the significance of Jesus for them in religious thought and practice.[28]

Devotion preceded and prompted doctrine. The joy felt in knowing Jesus may have defied expression but the passionate faith and love which lay behind it refused to settle for a dark mystery and pressed for articulation in Christology and council and creed. This ardour sustained the participants as they struggled to define Christian orthodoxy and from our viewpoint sweetens the story.

So Hurtado concludes, after nearly 700 pages of his study:

> The story of devotion to Jesus in earliest Christianity shows that the struggle erupted, volcano-like, at an amazingly early point. Probably, the continuing vitality of Christianity will remain dependent upon how fully Christians engage the question of Jesus, and how radically they are willing to consider what devotion to him means for them.[29]

Such joy in believing and loving and theologising is touched with the glint of coming glory, and so prophetic singers and poets and preachers continue to be needed to open 'the eyes of the heart' to the wonder of the unseen but not unknowable Jesus.

Faith as fervent and focused as this has its final *reward* (1:9). Why settle for anything less than heaven's best – which is salvation, experienced now and even more so in the future? Peter's mind brims with the wonder of it.

1:10–13 Salvation in three tenses

[10]Concerning this salvation, the prophets, who spoke of the grace that was to come to you, searched intently and with the greatest care,

[11]trying to find out the time and circumstances to which the Spirit of Christ in them was pointing when he predicted the sufferings of Christ and the glories that would follow. [12]It was revealed to them that they were not serving themselves but you, when they spoke of the things that have now been told you by those who have preached the gospel to you by the Holy Spirit sent from heaven. Even angels long to look into these things.

Be Holy

[13]Therefore, prepare your minds for action; be self-controlled; set your hope fully on the grace to be given you when Jesus Christ is revealed.

'*Salvation*' is a comprehensive term pointing to an experienced reality not to be missed and well worth waiting for. Concerning this 'salvation', Peter reminds us that it is being *prepared for the future* (cf 1:4–5,9).

Grace that has come (1:10) is still to come (1:13).

The salvation that in the present time faith now grasps (1:9) remains in large measure still to be experienced in the last time (1:5).

This salvation was *previewed by the prophets* (1:10–12). The burden of the prophets was the 'sufferings and subsequent glories of the Christ' (cf Luke 24:25,27). They 'searched intently' and were not mindless dreamers or mystics. Yet they spoke more than they knew and were in love with God enough to want to know the outcome of their prophecies.

They asked 'What?' and 'What kind of time?' their prophecies referred to. They strove, in word and deed, by poetry and vision, to give expression to the paradoxical blend of suffering and glory instilled in them by the Messianic Spirit (cf 2 Pet. 1:20–21). As seers, they previewed God's revelation of His secret strategy and plans for salvation.

Their testimony reinforces the conviction that salvation is no afterthought on God's part, no 'plan-B', but represents His precreation commitment to redeem whatever the world in its God-given freedom might come to.

This salvation is *preached by the apostles* in the present in the power of the Holy Spirit.

Wasn't it Peter who had the high privilege of being the first to say, '*this ... is that ...*'? *This* Easter event which we announce is *that* which the prophets heralded (Acts 2:16). Now we see that in the marvellous mystery of God's providence everything the prophets said was *for us* and our benefit (1:12). The gospel came to us in the power of the same Spirit who inspired the prophets. It was told to us by men who gave their lives to bring the message to us.

In the words of C.H. Spurgeon, 'The prophets foretold what the apostles reported. The seers looked forward and the evangelists look backward; their eyes meet at one place; they see eye to eye and both behold the cross.'

Nor is it only mortals who are transfixed by the sight.

Such a spectacle is *probed by angels*, peered into by heavenly beings (1:12) who have never seen anything like this: that the high King of heaven should forfeit His glory and win it again by suffering.

In J.B. Phillips' lovely parable, ours is the 'visited planet', and heaven lost its centre of attraction when Christ came to earth!

Christians living at the edge of society, feeling vulnerable and expendable, can take heart from this angelic curiosity. Wayne Grudem writes:

> Though the world may think such Christians insignificant and worthy of pity or scorn, angels – who see ultimate reality from God's perspective – find them to be objects of intense interest, for they know that these struggling believers are actually the recipients of God's greatest blessings and honoured participants in a great drama at the focal point of universal history.[30]

Peter has rehearsed the reasons for Christian hope in what has already happened: our *receiving mercy* which has given us *rebirth* into a living hope through the *resurrection of Jesus* from the dead. Now he urges us to fix that hope firmly on the grace to be given to us at the future *revelation of Jesus Christ* (1:13).

In Jürgen Moltmann's words, 'Just as the resurrection faith is hope's foundation, so Christ's second coming defines hope's horizon.'[31]

What is there to look forward to?

Christian, you will get what's coming to you, and what's coming to you is grace!

So we are orientated to the future. Set free from the past, we do not settle for a short-term view. We can afford to take the long view. Hope is our vantage point.

Edward Wilson was Scott's dying companion in Antarctica after their abortive attempt to beat Amundsen to the South Pole in 1912. In his last diary entry, Scott wrote to Mrs Wilson: 'I should like you to know how splendid he was at the end ... his eyes have a comfortable blue look of hope and his mind is peaceful with the satisfaction of his faith in regarding himself as part of the great scheme of the Almighty.'

Believers already participate in God's future. Hope is the tingling confidence that this is so.

Some people are natural optimists, others natural pessimists; for some the cup is always half full, for others it's always half empty. But living hope has nothing to do with this.

Such hope is a gift from God. It is not a passing mood, still less a personality trait, but a convinced outlook on life. It enables us to look reality – however harsh – firmly in the face without succumbing to despair. It is a firm stance in which our eyes are fixed on true and certain realities. In a determined orientation based on the grace we have already received, we 'set our hope fully on the grace to be given us when Jesus Christ is revealed'. In this way, in Jonathan Wilson's words, 'Hope becomes the habitual way of life for those who see their lives stretched between Christ's first and second coming.'[32]

Hopefulness is not wishful thinking, though exerting mental energy is vital. It is not escapism, though we are saved by hope.

Hope is not fantasising, though a sanctified imagination is essential. Hope reaches out for that grace to be revealed which will complement and perfect it.

Our deepest hopes and longings exist only because there also exists up ahead that for which our hearts long and dream and which is worthy of those desires and dreams. The extent of our hope is a measure of our human dignity and potential.

Despair is inhuman.

But hope is not a sentimental stance or an easy virtue. In an unredeemed world, it is salted with divine discontent which makes us thirsty for God's future. It calls for a deliberate and mindful protest against resignation to the way things are. 'Gird up the loins of your mind,' says Peter (1:13, AV), as a man with a long cloak must do if he is to spring into action. As we might now say, 'Roll up the sleeves of your mental processes,' and get ready for some active thinking.

Stay alert and spiritually aware. 'Be self-controlled', be 'sober', staying well balanced. Don't be intoxicated, today, by a commercial culture which wants to stop you thinking straight so that you go on consuming. It's in the interests of a 'fast-food culture' to cloud your judgment so that you stop thinking long-term, whether with historical perspective or prophetic vision. Materialism will shrink your soul and tame your spirit. But 'living hope' will expand the horizons of your heart.

Prayer and Reflection

We relish, Lord, the *living* hope we are newly born to:

> *hope* that is
> no mirage in the desert,
> no 'smoke-and-mirrors' illusion,
> no sleight-of-hand deception,
>
> but
> *hope* that is sure and certain,
> funded by Your resurrection,
> arising from the ashes of our broken dreams,
> *hope*
> fixed on Your return,
> already anchored in Your future.

Though we cannot see You, our love is not blind.
Where sight eludes us, trust hangs on to You.
When words fail us, our joy speaks for us.

Do good to us, Lord, even in our grieving.
Make better of us even in our refining.
Pray for us, Lord, that our faith fail not in the testing.

For we are glad to be Your Trinity-people, enfolded in Your love,
and these things we ask in that threefold name.
Amen.

- Examine your hopes and fears and lay them out before the
  Lord in prayer, asking the Holy Spirit to refocus your hopes on
  God's victory in Jesus – in His dying, rising and returning.

- Consider how Peter's message might strengthen our sense of identity in a society where Christians are increasingly marginalised and overlooked.

GOD'S PEOPLE DARE TO BE AS DIFFERENT AS GOD

1 PETER

1:14–16 Father's look-alike children

> [14]As obedient children, do not conform to the evil desires you had when you lived in ignorance. [15]But just as he who called you is holy, so be holy in all you do; [16]for it is written: 'Be holy, because I am holy.'

Christians are born again to be the *Father's look-alike children* (1:14–16).

Ultimately, Christian ethics is based on answers to the question 'What is God like?' Theology shapes character and behaviour and virtue. The charter for Israel as the people of God was 'Be holy, because I am holy' (Lev. 11:44). Holiness is what makes God, God; God is set apart, other, different.

But although God is 'wholly other', He does not keep His cosmic distance from us. The Holy One has made Himself known as the 'Holy One of Israel'. 'Be holy, because I am holy' is a covenant-making declaration, as faith-building as it is intimidating.

God calls us to share in His *holy differentness*. 'God's holiness,' asserts John Webster, 'cannot be isolated from God's calling of a people. God's holiness is actual as election to covenant.'[33] Born different we are to become so; God is the measure of how different we are to become!

Our growing conformity to God is matched by a non-conformity to the culture where it threatens our integrity as God's people (1:14). We are called to grow into the family likeness of the God who has given us new birth.

In his classic work on the subject of holiness the great Victorian bishop, J.C. Ryle, placed this at the head of his outline: 'Holiness is the habit of being of one mind with God, according as we find His mind described in Scripture. It is the habit of agreeing with God's judgement, hating what He hates, loving what He loves, and measuring everything in this world by the standard of His Word …'[34]

In Jim Packer's view, the call to holiness is one the contemporary evangelical Church urgently needs to hear: 'The shift of Christian interest away from the pursuit of holiness to focus on fun and fulfilment, ego-massage and techniques for personal success, and public issues that carry no challenge to one's personal morals … is, to my mind, a sad and scandalous fact that needs to be reversed.'[35]

Holiness, not gifts, ministry, personal success or mystical experiences, is the sign of true spiritual health. Such holiness is the mark not of the weird and eccentric and odd but of those fighting the good fight to become again truly human. In them the restoration of the defaced image of God in us is underway and gathering pace (cf Col. 3:10).

Developing such holiness of character is not an escapist venture into some monastic retreat. Rather, it is forged on the anvil of life's practical duties and relationships as workers, wives, husbands, parents, and friends. It is what Bonhoeffer called 'worldly holiness'.

This is not a matter of conforming to an outward ideal but of bending one's whole life to the shape of the new life we have been given. As Oswald Chambers once commented, 'By sanctification the Son of God is formed in me, then I have to transform my natural life into a spiritual life by obedience to Him.'

1:17 Fear that takes God seriously

Our commitment to be holy like God is suffused with a fear that takes God seriously. A holy person, wrote Bishop Ryle, 'will follow after the fear of God. I do not mean the fear of a slave, who only works because he is afraid of punishment and would be idle if he did not dread discovery. I mean rather the fear of a child, who wishes to live and move as if he was always before his father's face, because he loves him.'[36]

We are 'exiles' in every sense. Whatever pressures we face to conform to the godlessness around us, a holy fear acts as a moral antiseptic.

The fear of the Lord is the beginning of a wisdom that tells us that what seems to make sense in the short-term of the 'little while' (1:6) makes no sense at all in the long-term perspective of eternity. This healthy fear prevents us praying 'Our Father' in a way that is superficial or sentimental. Whereas familiarity breeds contempt, this is the respectful intimacy that calls on God as holy Father whose name is to be hallowed.

The biblical holiness of God's reborn children models what redeemed human life looks like. It embodies the paradox that obedience to the Father is perfect freedom.

Peter now traces our new-found freedom to the drastic effect upon us of Jesus in His death on the cross.

1:18–21 Freedom from futility through the cross

[18]For you know that it was not with perishable things such as silver or gold that you were redeemed from the empty way of life handed down to you from your forefathers, [19]but with the precious blood of Christ, a lamb without blemish or defect. [20]He was chosen before the creation of the world, but was revealed in these last times for your sake. [21]Through him you believe in God, who raised him from the dead and glorified him, and so your faith and hope are in God.

Through the cross we are freed from futile behaviour and cultural patterns inherited from the past. The liberation theology of the Bible is couched – as is Peter's message here – in the language of *redemption* derived from the exodus of the Israelites from Egypt. 'To redeem' is to purchase freedom for someone enslaved in some way by the payment of a price.

In the modern world, perhaps the ransom paid for the release of hostages is the nearest equivalent. But in the ancient world of Israel, payment was not in monetary terms but in blood. Their rescue from the Egypt that was enslaving them was by the blood of an unblemished lamb (Exod. 12–13). Seeing this blood, God's avenging angel of death 'passed over' the Israelite homes. For ever afterwards, this foundational saving event was commemorated in the Feast of Passover.

Drawing on this rich redemptive tradition, and with added echoes of Isaiah 53, Jesus Himself spoke movingly of His own mission: 'For even the Son of Man did not come to be served, but to serve, and to give his life as a *ransom* for many' (Mark 10:45).

The 'ransom price' was, as Peter vividly says, not perishable commodities such as gold or silver but something of infinite value – the precious blood of Christ, the unblemished Passover Lamb (1:18–19).

A theology of 'blood' has become unfashionable in our modern world, discarded by its enemies as a gruesome relic of primitive ritual practice or sentimentalised by its friends into clichéd piety.

For all its mistreatment, the image speaks of a violent death in which blood was shed. In Jesus' case, His 'blood' draws its meaning from being the climax of the long history of redemption. His 'blood' is not valueless or wasted but is 'precious', being invested with sacrificial and substitutionary significance. It therefore carries saving and redemptive weight. From what does the Lamb's blood free us? From sin, of course, but in particular, says Peter, 'from the empty way of life handed down to you from your forefathers' (1:18b).

The word Peter uses here, *mataios*, translated 'empty' (NIV) or better 'futile' (NRSV), is the same word used by the Septuagint in Ecclesiastes where the weary sage looks out on an unsatisfying world and exclaims, 'Vanity ... vanity ... all is vanity' or 'Meaningless! Meaningless! ... Everything is meaningless' (Eccles. 1:2, AV, NIV). These are habitual courses of actions, inherited mindsets, that provide no lasting direction and do not lead to life.

We are all born in bondage to the past. We arrive as damaged goods, we inherit patterns of conditioned behaviour. And the long shadow of genetic determinism looms over us all.

If this were not serious enough, we imbibe all kinds of cultural toxins with our mother's milk. These are the 'empty ways' we adopt simply through being born in a particular place and time to particular people. We breathe the air of our social environment; we imbibe the educational ideals we are taught; we conform to one degree or another with society's norms and expectations.

What is wrong with these inherited ways is precisely that there is no future in them, certainly none of God's future. They perhaps represent the equivalent for Gentile Christians of 'acts that lead to death' for Jewish Christians (cf Heb. 9:14).

'Futile ways' implies the primary socialisation of the believers before their conversion into the values, the world-view and religions of the dominant culture. It includes accepted and customary ways of behaving (cf 4:3).

But the blood of Jesus has enormous redemptive power. His death, as we embrace it in faith, breaks the shackles of the past, frees us from our cultural 'Egypt', and so gives us new and living hope of a new life and career. Through the cross I find blessed release from my old, self-determined, desire-driven, ignorant approach to life (1:14) which proved unfulfilling and wasted my human potential.

The cross sets us free from false ways of understanding freedom itself! Stanley Hauerwas writes, 'The project of modernity was to produce people who believe that they should have no story except the story they choose when they had no story. Such a story is called the story of freedom and is assumed to be institutionalised economically in market capitalism and politically in democracy.'[37]

The Christian gospel offers an alternative story. How novel it sounds to modern Western ears to be told that human self-fulfilment should entail the death of self and submission to the authority of grace in the gospel. As John Webster notes, 'The polarization of freedom and obedience that is endemic in modern anthropology is part of the pathology of the modern spiritual history of the self.'[38] It is precisely one of the 'futile ways' from which we need to be delivered by the cross. Evangelical freedom is 'a strange gift because it can only be known and exercised as we are converted from a lie – the lie that liberty is unformed and unconstrained self-actualization ... Evangelical freedom is thus freedom from the powers that inhibit me (including, and especially, my own powers).'[39]

In this way the forgiven have a future!

Hopes of freedom are realised through the death of Jesus Christ. Our hope in God 'is built on nothing less than Jesus' blood and righteousness'. In Paul Minear's words, 'The in-God-ness of hope is identical with its through-Christ-ness' (1:21).[40]

Prayer and Reflection

Holy Father,
Keep us in the healthy fear that prevents us being overfamiliar
with You.
Keep us in the wholesome freedom that matches words and deeds.

We thank You that Your Son's cross has set us free from
accustomed ways; ways that
    filled our time but drained life of meaning,
    made us feel better about ourselves but never connected
    us with You,
    promised life in the fast lane but proved to be dead ends.

We rejoice in our redemption in being
    rescued by His self-giving when given up for lost,
    ransomed by His blood when held hostage to sin,
    revalued by the price He paid for us.

Holy Father, there is no alternative to You,
There is really no alternative.
We have no choice but You if we are to be free.
Born free, sustain us in the glorious liberty of the children
    of God.
This we pray in Jesus' name.
Amen.

- Review the 'futile ways' from which you have been freed by
  Christ's death.
- Consider how different is the Christian view of freedom from
  that of the society in which you live.

GOD'S PEOPLE LIVE DIFFERENTLY TOGETHER

1 PETER

1:22-25 Purified by truth for love

[22]Now that you have purified yourselves by obeying the truth so that you have sincere love for your brothers, love one another deeply, from the heart. [23]For you have been born again, not of perishable seed, but of imperishable, through the living and enduring word of God. [24]For,

> 'All men are like grass,
>> and all their glory is like the flowers of the field;
> the grass withers and the flowers fall,
>> [25]but the word of the Lord stands forever.'

And this is the word that was preached to you.

The detoxifying of pagans, of course, is a deep process. Peter calls it a *'purifying of the soul'* (1:22, AV). This entails the progressive cleansing of our personality of wrong attitudes, old hurts and memories of past sins.

What we are purified for is *sincere love by obedience to the truth of the gospel.* The key signature of a holiness like God's is love for others. And this is achieved in us not by emotional experiences but by obedience to God's commands. God's Word, which creates life within us, carries with it the power as we obey it to promote the very life of God in us. 'Liberated from wilful and fearful self-seeking, I am consecrated for works of love.'[41]

Our souls are purified, our minds renewed and our love grows as we are continuously taught the truth and, more importantly, as we obey the truth – the truth of what God expects of us as His holy people, but above all the truth of what God has achieved in the death and resurrection of Jesus to set us free.

A holy Church is an attentive Church, which translates the Word into discipleship. The gospel is not only the initial power which gives us new life. Our lives are now to be shaped by a continual hearing of the gospel. 'The Church's holiness is visible as it hears afresh the promise and command of the gospel ... The Church is holy as a hearing Church.'[42]

The 'new birth' – which is elsewhere attributed to the action of the Holy Spirit (John 3:3ff.) – is here said to brought about by the 'seed' of God's Word. It is difficult to decide whether the image of seed implies raising plants or human procreation (this latter is perhaps more likely, though note verse 24 says 'all men are like grass ...'). Either way the point is made that this seed implants its own nature which is imperishable (*aphthartos*).

Isaiah had encouraged the exiles in Babylon in his day by assuring them that the vaunted permanence of their contemporary Babylon could not withstand the storm wind of God's Spirit nor outlive the powerful and enduring Word of the living Lord who alone shapes history (Isa. 40:6–8). So, writing from Rome, his contemporary 'Babylon', the self-styled 'eternal city', Peter eagerly echoes the prophet's confidence about what lasts.

Civilised life, however much it is buttressed by imperial blessings, is but a frail blade of grass, easily cut off in its greenness and soon to wither and die. So was our Redeemer, a tender shoot rooted in dry ground, scythed down in His prime. But 'from the ground there blossoms red, life that shall endless be'. And through the Word of His dying and rising there has been implanted into us a seed of His eternal, death-defying, indestructible life.

This seed of God's Word is nothing other than the *very gospel preached and passed down to us by the apostles of Christ* (1:25).

2:1–3 Purified by grace for growth

¹Therefore, rid yourselves of all malice and all deceit, hypocrisy, envy, and slander of every kind. ²Like newborn babies, crave pure spiritual milk, so that by it you may grow up in your salvation,

[3]now that you have tasted that the Lord is good.

By the continuous application of the Word of the gospel we are *purified for growth*.

Peter's exhortation brings to mind a mother reading the riot act to her fractious children at dinner time! Watch your table manners ... stop bickering ('rid yourselves of all malice') ... have you lost your appetite? ... you already drink too many fizzy drinks ... eat up your cabbage ... no, we're not having burgers again ('crave pure spiritual milk').

Christians are called to forego spiritual 'junk food' and over-sweet snacks. Christian progress is training the spiritual tastebuds to appreciate the satisfying goodness and nourishing grace of the Lord. 'Church growth' in the New Testament has little to do with the modern concern for numbers and evangelism and much more to do with developing love and godlikeness in community. Nourishment by the Word, feeding on truth, is the most vital factor for a healthy growing church.

2:4-8 Privileged with a threefold purpose

[4]As you come to him, the living Stone – rejected by men but chosen by God and precious to him – [5]you also, like living stones, are being built into a spiritual house to be a holy priesthood, offering spiritual sacrifices acceptable to God through Jesus Christ. [6]For in Scripture it says:

'See, I lay a stone in Zion,
    a chosen and precious cornerstone,
and the one who trusts in him
    will never be put to shame.'

[7]Now to you who believe, this stone is precious. But to those who do

not believe,

> 'The stone the builders rejected
> has become the capstone,'

[8]and,

> 'A stone that causes men to stumble
> and a rock that makes them fall.'

They stumble because they disobey the message – which is also what they were destined for.

An individualistic Western mindset has so infected evangelicalism that until recently we have paid little attention to developing a doctrine of the Church. Peter here offers us the foundation for such reflection.

The primary movement, as always, is *towards Christ* (2:4). Every movement of divine grace intends to move us further towards and into Christ. This is true of all things universally (Eph. 1:10), and of believers in being personally transformed (Rom. 8:28). It is also true of believers corporately as they constitute the Church (cf Eph. 4:13). This is Peter's concern here.

'As you come to him' translates the phrase in the Greek text *pros hon proserchomai*. E.G. Selwyn suggests that the double use of the preposition *pros* intensifies the sense of 'coming to Christ with a view to staying and becoming an adherent'.[43]

This may be an echo of Psalm 34 which seems to be in Peter's mind as he writes the letter (eg 2:3; 3:10ff.). The psalmist says that they are 'radiant' who 'draw near to Him' (*proselthate pros auton*, Psa. 34:5a, Septuagint). Those who do come find that 'their faces are never covered with shame' (Psa. 34:5b) – which anticipates the force of the quotation of Isaiah 40:6–8 in 1 Peter 2:6.

Every move we make in coming to faith and in ongoing

obedience is a coming to Christ, *'the living Stone'*. 'Living hope ... living word ... living Stone' – everything in Peter's vision of the gospel is an 'implied contrast with the hopelessness and idolatry of contemporary paganism'.[44]

Christ is 'the living Stone', hewn from the rock face of death by resurrection and raised high by ascension, who communicates His own vitality to us who believe.

What a wonderful paradox: *life* – all that is fluid, dynamic, empowering, fiery, growing, moving, developing – combined with *Stone* – that which is solid, enduring, reliable, unshifting, unyielding, immoveable!

So is the *Word* of this Lord: permanent and enduring but not a static statement; a gospel Word fresh with ever-breaking news, and life-giving potency.

It is the Word of *this Lord* who, as the living Stone, combines maximum vitality with maximum stability.

What God thinks of Him has made all the difference to His story. A career of noble failure is transmuted into strange success. God's estimate of Him proved decisive, and the imagery is drawn directly from Psalm 118:22.

Jesus was 'rejected' by the expert religious builders as not central to the 'house of God' they were erecting (2:4b). But God reversed the verdict men had passed on His Son and made Him the very central part of the edifice He is constructing. The One whom men deselected, God chose. The One whom men humiliated and shamed, God has elevated to the place of highest honour and glory. This was entirely of the Lord's doing and it is marvellous in our eyes

To this Christ we come, allowing ourselves in an inescapable movement of grace to be *built together* (2:5a). Drawn to the 'living Stone' we are inevitably drawn together as living building blocks. Our risky moves towards each other in Christ are as evangelical as our initial 'coming to Christ' in conversion. In fact it is impossible to do the one without doing the other. To come to Christ is to come to Christ as embodied in His Church. We come as 'living stones' to be built around the 'living Stone'.

There is a possible play on words here in which Peter perhaps makes an ironic point at his own expense. *Petros* is the word for an unworked piece of rock, rough-hewn and with jagged edges. But *lithos* – the word found in verses 4 and 5 – is used of stone which has been worked on by a stonemason so that it can fit alongside other pieces in a building.

Peter is a prime example of the kind of character, originally so angular and sharp-edged, that has to be chipped or even battered in shape by circumstances in order to work alongside others in Christ's Church. What is being built when we come together is God's 'building'. We are built together not merely for our own social reasons but *for* Him. It is not fellowship, however wonderful, or the mutual help and support it provides, which is the goal of our coming together. Rather, it is to be His house, a God-indwelt community where He is at home and where people who know His address can find Him!

This is the essential *Godward orientation* of the Church, which has three aspects to it: 'spiritual house … holy priesthood … spiritual sacrifices' (2:5).

Believers, firstly, constitute *'a spiritual house'*. God's people no longer orientate to the one Temple in Jerusalem, however splendid. By the time Peter was writing, this symbolic edifice was either under threat or already destroyed. But all that the literal Temple aimed to be – a meeting place of heaven and earth, God and His people – so the Church centred on the living reality of Christ is intended to be in every place.

What is envisaged is a temple of people, built into Christ, inspired and operating by the presence and power of God the Holy Spirit. Here is a recipe for the continuous reformation and revival of the Church. Church history shows only too clearly how each generation needs to take Peter's prescription to heart. Our history tells us, sadly all too frequently, how easily the life of the

Church hardens into an unyielding institution, impervious even to God's own intrusion.

I worship currently with Anglicans but I have non-conformity in my blood. My ecclesiological roots are Baptist and Pentecostal and charismatic. But I know only too well from personal experience how every one of these brands of churchmanship is prone to a 'hardening of the categories'. Peter's word is always in season.

Without the Spirit, movements quickly become monuments. Too often the Church takes the 'spiritual' for granted and presses on with its man-made programmes. As Bishop John Taylor wryly observed in his celebrated book on the Holy Spirit, 'I have not heard recently of committee business adjourned because those present were still awaiting the arrival of the Spirit of God. I have known projects abandoned for lack of funds, but not for lack of the gifts of the Spirit.'[45]

In a book which my father pressed on me when I was still a teenager, the famous Methodist preacher of an earlier generation, Samuel Chadwick, wrote, 'To run an organisation needs no God. Man can supply the energy, enterprise and enthusiasm for things human. The real work of the Church depends upon the work of the Holy Spirit.'[46]

It is vital to add that this description of the Christian community as a 'house' has wider communal as well as more specific cultic dimensions in view. The Church – if we may put it like this – is a dwelling-place not only for God but for His people and for God-with-His-people. Those people in society, now believers in Christ, who have no special place, no distinctive cultural identity and anchorage, now together form a new 'house' which is their home.

As that 'spiritual house' believers constitute, secondly, a *'holy priesthood'* set apart for God and His will in the world.

A priest is one who has special access to God and acts as an intermediary in the worship of God's people.

In the largest sense, it is Jesus, and Jesus alone, as our High Priest who fulfils these functions for us. In His death on the cross, He has made the one true sacrifice for sins and made it once-for-all. In His ascended heavenly ministry, He is now the mediator between us and God, interceding for us and representing us before the throne of God.

Our priesthood derives from His finished and ongoing priestly work and is subordinate to it.

Old Testament priesthood was a carefully prescribed office, open only to those from one tribe in Israel who underwent scrupulous preparation prior to ordination (cf Exod. 28).

We have the privilege of all being what only a few were in that previous era of grace. The 'priesthood of all believers' is a precious reality that must not be suffocated by necessary but over-obtrusive leadership nor trivialised by an anarchic and self-indulgent enthusiasm.

Our priestly task is to offer *sacrifices* to God. We do not repeat the sacrifice of the cross – as some cruder forms of Catholicism construe from what goes on in the Mass. We do not replicate His self-offering but respond in the good of it.

The 'sacrifices' offered by this holy priesthood are 'spiritual'. As with 'a spiritual house', the adjective 'spiritual' does not denote what is non-material but what is energised and charged with the Holy Spirit.

The Old Testament worship patterns echoed here, however, transposed into new covenant realities, nevertheless strike at the heart of our self-interest in being Christians. Worship in these terms is not reducible to religious therapy or entertainment. Nor is worship confined to what happens when the congregation gathers to praise and pray.

If we ask 'What are our spiritual sacrifices?' the New Testament offers us a variety of answers: giving money (Phil. 4:18), praising God in worship (Heb. 13:15), doing good works (Heb. 13:16), witness and ministry (Rom. 15:16) – in short, the offering of our whole lives to God for our minds to be renewed and non-conformist ways of living to be shown in our lives (Rom. 12:1ff.). Every facet of life is set alight by a spark from the fire of Christ's own sacrifice on the cross.

All this is meant to be 'acceptable to God', not to society or Church growth experts or trendy theorists! Jesus makes everything we offer acceptable to His Father.

Christ, the 'living Stone', is the centrepiece of this spiritual house. Everything we offer to God is 'through Jesus Christ'.

The centrality of Jesus to all that God is building is underlined by Peter's quotation of the prophet Isaiah. The description of Jesus as the 'cornerstone' again echoes Psalm 118:22 and directly cites Isaiah 28:16.

In ancient construction methods, a cornerstone

- controls the way a building is erected since everything is built out from it as the starting point and
- is visible (unlike a foundation stone).

Is it obvious that Jesus controls everything in your life or determines the shape and development of your church?

2:6–8 The crucial difference between us is Christ Himself

It is our being a Christ-centred community that distinguishes us from the unbelieving world around us.

I recall sitting next to a charming and urbane Muslim businessman on a flight to Karachi. I noticed that he wanted to write something but couldn't find his pen and so lent him mine. This opened up a friendly conversation. He graciously refused to eat his 'kosher' airline meal until mine had arrived somewhat later and pressed me to stop over in Pakistan to accept his hospitality for a few days. A long discussion ensued about Christianity and Islam. With all the issues we gently argued about or skirted round we arrived at every turn at the Person of Jesus Himself – and found that He was our chief bone of contention!

So it always proves. Jesus is our greatest attraction and the greatest offence. In the end, He cannot be avoided. He is either a stepping-stone to God as you believe or a stumbling-block to those who disobey the Word – none of which, Peter assures us, lies outside the mysterious wisdom and strange sovereignty of God.

Peter is not writing a systematic or philosophical statement, much less a theodicy. Rather, his goal is to comfort the beleaguered Christians in Asia Minor by telling them that even their situation of experiencing hostility from the culture is not outside the scope of God's plans.

The modern Western world has been characterised as a 'culture of death'. Isaiah 28 describes just such a culture in which the official leaders of the nation have made a 'pact with the grave', buttressed by lies and falsehood (Isa. 28:15). It is precisely in the midst of a world in love with death and deceit that God establishes Jesus as a 'tested stone, a precious cornerstone, a sure foundation' of a new society in which truth and justice flourish (Isa. 28:16–17).

Those who in desperate faith run for refuge to the living Stone may be lowly in the esteem of a smart society and count for little. But in God's estimation, His people who believe in Christ share in the value and honour He gives to Jesus (2:7).

The much-loved and traditional translation of the Authorised Version – 'unto you ... which believe he is precious' – is almost certainly incorrect. It borrowed the adjective 'precious' from verse 4 when in fact Peter uses the noun here – *timē* – meaning honour or value.

The passage from Isaiah 28 which Peter has just quoted ends with the pledge that the one who 'trusts in him will never be put to shame'. Now Peter states this reassurance in positive terms: honour belongs to those who put their faith in God's precious Son, Jesus Christ.[47]

'Exiles and aliens' who are nameless and powerless 'nobodies' in society's reckoning are in fact 'somebodies' – the very people of God. The honour is ours as believers of being His royal priesthood, His holy nation, and finally of being vindicated by God in glory and honour (1:7).

2:9–10 Privileged with a fourfold identity

> [9]But you are a chosen people, a royal priesthood, a holy nation, a people belonging to God, that you may declare the praises of him who called you out of darkness into his wonderful light. [10]Once you were not a people, but now you are the people of God; once you had not received mercy, but now you have received mercy.

It is hard for modern readers to feel the radical force of the move Peter is making here. He bestows on the whole Christian community all the titles of privilege first given to Israel as God's covenant people (cf Exod. 19:3–6).

Christian believers are *chosen* in the 'chosen One' (cf 2:4). We are joined as believers in Christ to the gracious origin, covenant relationship and manifest destiny of Israel.

The Church is the developed and extended remnant of Israel. It does not replace Israel of old. Rather, Israel as the covenant people of God is reconstituted around a new centre, Jesus, who fulfils the law and replaces the Temple.

To anticipate Pauline language, we are grafted into the old stock (Rom. 11; Eph. 3:3ff.).

Do we realise who we are?

'Exiles and aliens' though we may be in sociological terms, counting for little in the empire's scheme of things, we are the people whom the one Creator God has chosen as His own.

We are chosen to be a *'royal priesthood'*. Priests enjoy privileged access to God, and so are able to intercede for people before God and to discern and declare God's will for people. They act as go-betweens linking God and the world. The traffic passes both ways.

A priestly people has a mediatorial role to bring God and the nations together. But it is the priesthood of the Church as a whole, not of any individual in it or even a collection of individuals. 'The church is the great *intermediary* between God and man, because it is in trust of the one saving Gospel of the great *Mediator*.'[48] Our mission is to bring Him to the world and the world to Him.

It is a *royal* priesthood because it is in the service of God's kingdom. Such a role transposes the original human vocation to exercise dominion into a higher key. It promises to rule the world through prayer and intercession and self-sacrifice.

The calling to be a *holy nation* accentuates the 'differentness' which we have seen is at the heart of Peter's pastoral aim.[49]

Again, Israel's privileged history carries a spiritual health warning. Sensing the need of a strong leader who could restore order in the chaotic end of the period of the judges, the people of Israel asked the prophet Samuel for a king – ironically so as to be, they said, like every other nation – a reason which struck at the very heart of Israel's unique vocation and destiny (1 Sam. 8:5).

In similar fashion, Jesus warned His disciples about taking their concepts of leadership from the management manuals of the pagans: it is 'not so with you' (Mark 10:42–45).

Peter's remarkable description of the Church urges the same attitude on his readers: 'Don't be the same as everyone else; dare to be as different as God is different.'

There really does exist on earth a form of human reality that corresponds to God's own uniqueness and holiness (cf 1:15–16).

'You are ... a *people belonging to God*.

This description, though sounding less romantic than the other terms, nonetheless encapsulates the astonishing transformation which is told in verse 10 in almost poetically symmetrical language: 'Once you were not a people ... now you are the people of God; once you had not received mercy ... now you have received mercy.' By God's 'great mercy' (1:3), 'nobodies' have become 'somebodies'.

Peter draws here on the prophet Hosea. The prophet speaks into a situation in which God had judged and repudiated a rebellious nation so that they became a 'non-people'.

Hosea, who became the living embodiment of God's suffering love, reassures God's rejected people of a new betrothal. 'I will show my love to the one I called "Not my loved one". I will say to those called "Not my people", "You are my people"; and they will say, "You are my God"' (Hosea 2:23).

Peter, like Paul, extends the scope of the 'non-people' to embrace Gentiles; and to them, as well as Jews, whether devout or rebellious, God has through the gospel extended His new covenant love (cf Rom. 9:24–25).

John Webster brings out the stark contrast and saving shock implicit in these words: 'Apart from God, human history is populated by that bleak, estranged and ruined company called "no people" … But ingredient within the gospel is the claim that there now exists the extraordinary fact of *laos theou*, people of God.'[50]

What great mercy!

We need to pause and reflect on this astonishing vision of the Church lest we are misled by its grandeur.

With election comes responsibility (cf Amos 3:2). Like Abraham, Israel existed to mediate the blessings of God to the wider world. As a direct result, there is slipped into the vocational charter of Israel given in Exodus 19:4–6 – almost in parenthesis – the crucial statement *'although the whole earth is mine'* (Exod. 19:5b).

As I have written elsewhere, 'Here is the most selective covenant arrangement imaginable, one that excludes the most powerful civilisations of the ancient world, like China and indeed Egypt. But right at the very heart of the process of choosing one nation is inserted the significant reminder that God's eyes are still on the whole earth. Israel is meant never to forget that her special privileges, exclusive status, are to serve God's plans for every nation and all His creation.'[51]

What was true of Israel, then, is truer still for the new covenant people of God. Our sense of chosenness and special privilege should not lead to exclusivism or an inward-looking self-congratulation. This is made clear by the reminder that the Church exists to 'declare the praises of him who called you out of darkness into his wonderful light'. Election is for purpose rather than privilege.

In Gerhard Lohfink's view, the concept of election 'has not the slightest thing to do with preference, advantage, elitism, or being better-than, but it has a great deal to do with God's respect for human dignity and freedom'. Commenting on the verses we are considering, Lohfink urges us to see that 'election is not something for its own sake and that it does not serve the self-realization of those who are chosen. Instead, these are chosen in order that they may be obedient to Jesus Christ and in order that they may proclaim the mighty deeds of God.'[52] This is a point well taken.

But such necessary warnings should never be allowed to rob us of the joy of knowing who we are in Christ.

The danger is less that we naively over-inflate the Church's ego to fill the space of these lofty epithets; rather, it is that we cynically shrink them to fit our current size.

Better, as William Abraham suggests, to treat these grand titles as 'veiled promises'. Our greatest danger, he insists, 'is that we take them flat-footedly and apply them to ourselves as we are and thus reduce them to what we find in our communities. What these images do evoke is a picture of what we can be when we allow the Holy Spirit to act fully among us. They display features of the church as it is meant to be in the power of the Holy Spirit.' So, he concludes, 'we do not give up if our church is now a country club, a Noah's ark, or a giant waterbed'. Instead we draw by faith on these titles as an 'amazing treasury of hope and a charter of a new creation'.[53]

These titles of privilege remain a source of wonder to all believers. They raise our sights and our hopes. To a church 'in exile' they are crucial.

We must never allow the culture to 'name' the Church. We should always risk identifying ourselves by the names and titles God gives in His grace. This is just another way in which we may show how free we are from the futile ways of describing us inherited from our society with its stereotypical and naturalistic labels for us. In Norman Kraus's words, we are no longer dependent on 'social roles, economic standards, minority-majority status, religious affiliation and ideological or political associations to confer individual identity and worth'.[54]

Don't let the world squeeze us into its mould – even its categories. Let's resist being caricatured by unbelief. Let us so live differently in truth and love that we baffle and confound all merely cultural attempts to define us. By grace let us allow ourselves to be defined and shaped by the gospel alone.

2:9b 'You are ... that you may ...'

Here in a nutshell is the amazing change the gospel has brought to our relationship with God.

The exilic prophets Jeremiah and Ezekiel promised a *new* covenant when the 'ought' and 'must' of the old covenant would be replaced through the Spirit with an *inner disposition* to obey God and to fulfil the requirement of His Torah. In short, the 'must' of 'you shall' would be replaced by 'you may'.

In a famous sermon preached in Basel prison, Karl Barth rightly discerned the new covenant overtones in Peter's words. He told the prisoners there:

If God puts this law, this command and this promise of His within you and writes it in your heart, then you may obey it. Then you *may* allow yourself to be loved, and then you *may* love Him in return – love Him, God, and as a result your neighbour also ...

You may: that is the new and true commandment, the law of God put within us and written in our hearts. Simply and straight-forward-ly it is our freedom to enjoy Him, and obediently to do His will.[55]

'You *are* ... that you *may* ...' Obligation and prescription is turned into freedom and permission! 'You are that you may' is our law of life.

The best evangelism is irresistible evangelism whose 'must' is the irrepressible testimony of those who 'cannot help speaking about what [they] have seen and heard' (Acts 4:20).

Our mission is validated by inevitable good works and credible behaviour which are the outcome of our worship as we declare to the world the virtues of our God in song and speech and holy living.

The priesthood of all believers is, for the same reason, the prophethood of all believers, the people God has formed for His praise (cf Isa. 43:21).

Praise is a repudiation of sin, and of sin's refusal to honour God in everything. If it can express itself humbly without being glibly triumphalistic:

- Praise dispels the fog of despair and offers genuine hope.
- Praise is characteristic of those who are marvelling in the light of God's saving deeds.
- Praise is the voice of those who are learning to see more clearly what is worthy and what is unworthy of our admiration.
- Praise singingly inverts the screwed-up values of a world into which, as William Temple once put it, someone has sneaked and 'swapped all the price tags'.
- Praise expresses prophetic discernment of what is truly valuable, lauding what should be esteemed and debunking what is idolatrous.

Whenever such praise overspills into the community it

becomes evangelism. Authentic witness is the inevitable overflow of worship. The mission of the Church consists of finding myriad ways of extolling the virtues of grace and inviting others to taste and see with us that the Lord is good.

Prayer and Reflection

Father God, we thank You for Your
living Word;
    grass withers,
    flowers fade,
    empires wax and wane
but
    Your Word lives on,
    Your 'text lingers',
    Your truth prevails,
    Your gospel stays preached.

Father God, we hasten to Your
living Stone;
    unto Him shall the gathering of God's people be,
    upon Him shall the Church be built,
    around Him shall the temple of the Lord grow.

This is Your doing, Lord God, and it is marvellous in our eyes. In making Jesus to be who He is, You have made *us* to be what we are:

By You we are *entitled*
    – the nobodies made somebodies,
By You we are *named*
    – irreducible to worldly definition and categorising,
By You we are *ennobled*

– identified as royal agents of a ruling God.
Much can be said to castigate and condemn Your Church.
But we are the people who have received Your mercy; what more
   needs to be said?
Your mercy is making something of us; what more can be
   expected of us?

So, Lord, teach us to keep our heads high and our hearts humble.
   Reverser of all lesser verdicts,
   Raiser from the dead,
   Exalter of the rejected,
   Vindicator of the oppressed,
   Source of living hope.
Amen.

- Reflect on all the ways in which God's Word nourishes
  your life.
- Consider how we might combat caricatures of the Church
  in the media and among our friends and workmates without
  painting an untrue picture of who we really are.

GOD'S PEOPLE BEHAVE DIFFERENTLY IN THE WORLD

1 PETER

2:11-12 Living differently as strangers

[11]Dear friends, I urge you, as aliens and strangers in the world, to abstain from sinful desires, which war against your soul. [12]Live such good lives among the pagans that, though they accuse you of doing wrong, they may see your good deeds and glorify God on the day he visits us.

We might see the Church Peter has envisioned so far as having *four characteristic movements:* towards Christ, towards one another, towards God and – this is what he now elaborates on – *towards the world.*

To 'exiles' (as 1:1) is added *paroikos,* translated variously as 'aliens' or 'strangers'.

Note that the NIV gratuitously inserts 'in the world' into the text so obscuring any social meaning and opting for a purely spiritual meaning. However, as we mentioned earlier, it is best to combine the sociological and religious meanings.

Paroikos – 'resident aliens' – carries the connotation of *legal status* whereas *parepidemos* – 'strangers' – conveys the transitory nature of their position in society.

Jesus spelled out the basic stance of His disciples as being in the world but not of the world (John 17:14–19). Our differentness stems from the reality of our new birth into a new life (1:3,23); we have a new point of origin, a new starting point for thinking and behaving, and a new destiny which fosters new hopes and dreams. Christians, then, live in a measure of *contrast* to the world. All of which make us different from our culture.

It is our freedom (cf 1:18) from established patterns and accepted norms that threatens others and rouses hostility. Free from 'peer pressure' we are free to act and react differently as *paroikos* and *parepidemos.*

It is intriguing and ironic that from *paroikos* we get the word 'parish' which was originally meant to highlight Christian distinctiveness, not Christian conformity!

Pressed to give answers, let us also be those who ask questions, especially awkward questions, of our society, and let us be among the first to be sceptical of easy answers.

We sometimes face unavoidable *conflict* with the world. Our 'sinful desires' seek to block the Spirit's work in our lives (2:11), and so we must engage in warfare against 'the world, the flesh and the devil'. We may well underestimate the reality of evil in the world and the way it afflicts our lives. Peter warns us to be alert to the devil's malevolence (5:8). Equally, we can overstate the role of the devil when the sharpest and nearest battle is with our own self-centredness and compromise with the culture!

Peter has the balance: flesh (2:11); world (4:1–4); devil (5:8–9) – all war against my soul.

Part of our fight is with deception. We have been sold a lie.

The deep conviction of the apostles – as of many great theologians since, such as Jonathan Edwards – is that our chief end is to glorify God and to enjoy Him for ever. Our true self-fulfilment and God's own pleasure and glory are not set on divergent but converging courses. Only the devil blinds us to seeing that doing God's will and living to His glory is the way of life designed by our Creator to satisfy our deepest needs and desires.

2:13–17 Living differently as subjects

[13]Submit yourselves for the Lord's sake to every authority instituted among men: whether to the king, as the supreme authority, [14]or to governors, who are sent by him to punish those who do wrong and to commend those who do right. [15]For it is God's will that by doing good you should silence the ignorant talk of foolish men. [16]Live as free men, but do not use your freedom as a cover-up for evil; live as servants of God. [17]Show proper respect to everyone: Love the brotherhood of believers, fear God, honour the king.

Be respectful of every lawful institution. Be sensitive to God's creation-order and not needlessly rebellious. This is Peter's firm exhortation.

Given the politico-social fabric of the day, the New Testament is nevertheless clear about the limits and role of government, namely to keep 'law and order' in society.

When such a role infringes on God's sovereignty we are at liberty to resist totalitarian idolatry (cf Acts 4:18–20; cf the book of Revelation). But we are not called to contribute to the lawlessness and general lack of respect for authority which is certainly prevalent today (2:17). We are free people but we are not anarchists. The motivation is crucial: 'for the Lord's sake' (2:13), as servants of God, act as free men (2:16).

This underlines where our ultimate allegiance lies. Sit loose to political idolatry of all kinds. Be prepared to be misunderstood by 'ignorant and foolish men' (2:15), but do your best patiently to minimise this – perhaps best of all by showing an exceptional concern for social justice.

Reflect for a moment on where Peter has brought us so far.

Christians are undoubtedly characterised by their 'newness'. We have been freed from the 'futile ways' inherited from our fathers, whatever forms that 'ancestor worship' may have taken.

By the good *news* of the gospel we have been given *new* birth as God's *new* covenant people already experiencing the vibrant and novel life of God's *new* creation.

At the same time, however, the Christian movement is not unprecedented but draws deeply on the age-old promises of God and is continuous with the long history of God's Old Testament people. Hence the grounding of the gospel in Old Testament prophecy (explicitly at 1:10–12; 1:24–25; 2:6–8; 2:22ff. etc) and the ascription to the Church of Israel's privileged titles and vocation (2:9–10).

Peter no doubt had good pastoral reasons for opting to stress this *continuity* with all that God has done before.

In Peter's day, novel ideas, new trends and the latest fads may have been attractive to philosophical speculators (cf Acts 17:19–21). But novelty was socially suspect. In the ancient world it was an advantage to be able to show that your movement had historic roots. Your group was more likely to be seen as credible if it could demonstrate connection with a long and noble heritage.

What the Church historian Robert Wilkin says about Roman attitudes in the second century is likely to have started about the time of Peter's writing. Wilkin observes:

> Given the attitude that religion is a patrimony from the past which sustains the life of the state, it was inevitable that the piety of the persecutors would conflict with the new movement which had begun in Palestine. The Christians were seen as religious fanatics, self-righteous outsiders, arrogant innovators who thought that only their beliefs were true.[56]

None of the apostles doubted that their beliefs were true. But all were at pains to urge upon the young movement a wisdom beyond its years learned only from the Holy Spirit.

Live boldly as free men but not exploiting your freedom needlessly to flout convention in socially irresponsible ways.

Be as different as God is but not self-righteously so.

Miroslav Volf comments wisely:

> Difference from a culture must never degenerate into a simple flight from the culture. Rather, to be alien and exile must be a way of living in a culture and for a culture. In biblical terminology, the kingdom of God is not of this world, but it is in this world and for this world. Distance must involve belonging as belonging must involve distance.[57]

First Peter would say to us, in effect: believe you are right, but be prepared to give reasons for the hope that you have, and do it 'with gentleness and respect'. Stand apart from society – not least morally and ethically – but let your distinctive character become visible in good works that pagans can see and, in the miraculous providence of God, approve of.

If the 'aliens' have landed and have turned out to be us, we have no need to 'alienate' our fellow citizens by being self-consciously oddball or gratuitously offensive.

The Church – in John Howard Yoder's striking phrase – is a 'social novelty of grace', but in communicating the novelty we will do well to emphasise and embody the grace!

Peter's word is increasingly applicable even to Christians in the post-Christendom Western world. More and more we find ourselves living as 'aliens', a beleaguered minority in an unbelieving culture. Our strangeness stands out, our differentness makes us awkward.

Not for one moment would Peter encourage us to disguise our differentness and compromise our integrity by assimilating with the culture. Quite the opposite.

Rather than bemoan our fate or become introverted and defensive, we may with grace and gumption turn our oddness into opening for mission and witness. As J.J. Elliott puts it, 'The social situation in which you exist, in other words, with all its implications of limitation and estrangement, is an opportunity and a challenge for you to manifest your holiness and allegiance to God.'[58]

2:18–20 Living differently as servants

[18]Slaves, submit yourselves to your masters with all respect, not only to those who are good and considerate, but also to those who are harsh. [19]For it is commendable if a man bears up under the pain of unjust suffering because he is conscious of God. [20]But how is it to your credit if you receive a beating for doing wrong and endure

it? But if you suffer for doing good and you endure it, this is commendable before God.

Here again is the honest realism and wisdom of the gospel. It is not so idealistic in a romantic sense that it cannot work even in the most oppressive societies.

The gospel has revolutionary consequences. But unlike some extreme forms of liberation theology in South America we should not conflate this with Marxism and be too ready to jump to anarchic conclusions from the freedom of the gospel.

Peter is not blind to what is 'unjust' (2:19) and is realistic in knowing how unreasonable bosses can be (2:18c). But his is wise counsel at a time when Christians did not have political power.

What is tragic is that when the Church did have such power – whether in eighteenth-century England or the American South – it chose for too long to perpetuate slavery.

Thankfully, also, we remember that it was the evangelical Christian conscience of William Wilberforce and others which eventually led the way to its abolition.

Peter's exhortation, then, is demanding but impressive. In extreme circumstances, even slaves – whose lives were otherwise so demeaning – are dignified with being responsible people free at least to react in a Christlike way. There is no situation, however oppressive or constricting, where it is not possible to follow Jesus in some way.

As I contemplate this text, I am conscious of being for the most part a long remove from the reality described. It is as if as a jumper the bar has been set too high.

But how can it be otherwise? Did not you and I sign up for the long haul and the full treatment whatever that entails?

There is only one road; it goes on and on for ever and, like a great river, its springs are at every doorstep and every path is its tributary. Going out of your door is a dangerous business, Frodo had been warned by Bilbo: 'You step into the Road, and if you don't keep your feet, there is no knowing where you might be swept off to.'[59]

Following Jesus – not withstanding every effort on our part to be gracious and gentle and humble to avoid offence – will almost certainly take us into hostile territory. In fact it is the Christ-lifestyle which is guaranteed to incite ridicule and rage.

The suffering Peter addresses is not deliberately chosen, as if it were some kind of hair-shirt asceticism. Here the pain is caused to slaves and is *unjust suffering*. This is suffering which is endured in full awareness of God (2:19b).

To endure suffering in this way is 'commendable' to God or better – and in a more literal translation – is 'a grace-gift from God' (2:19a,20b).[60] What Christian slaves endured and what all Christians may suffer in various ways is the inevitable consequence of our calling. 'To this you were called, because Christ suffered for you, leaving you an example, that you should follow ...'

2:21–25 The cross makes all the difference

[21]To this you were called, because Christ suffered for you, leaving you an example, that you should follow in his steps.

[22]'He committed no sin,
    and no deceit was found in his mouth.'

[23]When they hurled their insults at him, he did not retaliate; when he suffered, he made no threats. Instead, he entrusted himself to him who judges justly. [24]He himself bore our sins in his body on the tree, so that we might die to sins and live for righteousness; by his wounds you have been healed. [25]For you were like sheep going astray, but now you have returned to the Shepherd and Overseer of your souls.

Jesus' example is crucial to our understanding of our calling in the world. How He reacted and what He accomplished make all the difference to us.

As I write, Mel Gibson's controversial film on the passion of Christ is stirring debate and dividing opinions everywhere. Is it a shocking reminder of the brutal reality of crucifixion or is it a gratuitous assault on our sensitivities, an unrelenting torrent of violence that eventually numbs our feelings and obscures the saving message of the cross?

Is this a lapse into medieval Catholicism's almost masochistic obsession with the physical sufferings of Jesus which led the mystics to fixate on the wounds of Jesus and characteristically left a legacy of the crucifix with a pre-resurrected Christ still hanging there?

Do we become what Kierkegaard called 'professors of crucifixion'? Is this a kind of voyeurism? Were the evangelists right to be reticent about describing the physical details of such a gruesome event for fear of obscuring the meaning and the message? Is it possible to obliterate the grace with the gore?

No doubt in today's media-crazed world, a camera and microphone would have been thrust into the face of the tortured victim, asking Him how He was feeling!

'Were you there when they crucified my Lord …?'

Well, Peter was, as he reminds us, a 'witness of Christ's sufferings' (5:1). He is in no doubt that the cross is central to our gospel and our faith. Peter's viewpoint on this is a vital part of the New Testament's witness to the saving events of Easter.

Peter certainly does not shrink from the horrific reality of what crucifixion entailed. He prefers the word 'sufferings' to 'death' as if to recall the agonisingly drawn-out execution. He presents to us no stained-glass window version of the crucifixion. Instead he speaks in blunt terms of Jesus in His flesh-and-blood 'body' being fixed to a rough-hewn piece of timber which he calls the 'tree'. Yet even the stark word 'tree' may have theological resonances. Perhaps

Peter deliberately used the word to allude to the curse which the Torah prescribed for anyone hanging on a tree (Deut. 21:23; cf Gal. 3:13–14).

Crucifixion was unquestionably one of the most macabre and cruel forms of judicial killing ever invented. It was designed to prolong the agony of the sufferer to intolerable lengths. It exposed the naked victims to maximum public humiliation and degradation. The Romans reserved the punishment for special categories of offenders, including runaway slaves and political rebels against Rome.[61]

Peter, then, in no way presents to us an idealised or sanitised view of the cross.

Having said that, however, it seems clear that his chief interest is in celebrating the *meaning* of the crucifixion as a saving event. James Denney's words are wise:

> The death of Christ was never presented to the world as a spectacle. It was never presented by an apostle or evangelist apart from an interpretation. It was the death of Christ so interpreted as to appeal irresistibly to the heart, the conscience, the imagination, perhaps we should sometimes include the very senses of men, which exercised the emancipating power.[62]

Peter weaves a rich tapestry of reflection on the cross in which we can identity the following strands of atonement theology.

2:21 The cross of Christ *redirects our steps*
The death of Jesus is a crossroads for every one of us. No one can truly come to it and go away the same. To become His disciple is to take up our cross and follow Him. Coming to the cross is the turning-point of conversion. Meeting Jesus in His death changes the whole direction our lives are pointing in.

In His patient endurance of suffering, the Lord Jesus has left us an 'example'. The word *hupogrammon*, translated 'example', was used of the letters at the top of a page which a child in school was meant to copy in learning the alphabet. So our discipleship commits us to an A-to-Z involvement in the cruciform pattern of Jesus' life.

Following Jesus, in Martin Hengel's words, means 'unconditional *sharing of the master's destiny,* which does not stop even at deprivation and suffering in the train of the master …' This entails, as Hengel notes, 'complete trust on the part of the person who "follows"; he has placed his destiny and future in his master's hands'.[63]

Though it fits uneasily into a Protestant evangelical prospectus, the 'imitation of Christ' is a clear feature of apostolic teaching. No doubt it is possible to devalue the ideal by seeking to implement it in a wooden and literalistic way.

The logo 'WWJD?' recently became fashionable in the USA as a lapel badge or other piece of 'holy hardware'. The practice of asking 'What Would Jesus Do?' harks back to Charles Sheldon's Victorian novel, *In His Steps*. It would be easy to dismiss this current fad, as it would the book, as simplistic and sentimental. But, as Christian ethicist Allan Verhey says, it has the merit, at least, of not appealing to a set of abstract rules but of evoking the real and human Person of Jesus.

Biblical commentator J.N.D. Kelly suggests that Peter used the graphic 'footsteps' not so that we attempt to reproduce the details of Jesus' lifestyle in a culture and era far removed from His own but so that we might simply move in the same direction He chose to go. The cross reorientates the direction of our lives and sets us on a kingdom road.

For Jesus, the way of the cross was a 'must' He freely chose to accept; for us it is a 'call' which, likewise, we are invited freely to embrace.

In the old *Quo Vadis?* legend, Peter is fleeing Rome during the persecution of Christians under the emperor Nero. Along the Appian Way, as he is leaving the city, the big fisherman is stopped in his tracks by a vision of Jesus who is going in the opposite direction. *'Quo vadis, Domine?'* 'Where are You going, Lord?' Peter asks. And the vision answers, 'Into Rome, to be crucified again.' With that, Peter turns round and goes back to the burning city and – according to tradition – to his own upside-down crucifixion.

2:22-23 The cross *revokes the law of retaliation*

As He was without sin or deceit, Jesus Christ suffered *unjustly*. When insulted, He did not threaten revenge. However much He suffered, He never threatened violence in return.

His passion was the intensification of earlier wounding provocations – what the writer to the Hebrews called the 'opposition from sinful men' (Heb. 12:3).

People smirked at His humble origins and behind His back joked about the mystery surrounding His birth. 'Nazareth! Can anything good come from there?' (John 1:46). 'How can the Christ come from Galilee?' (John 7:41–42). The slurs cut deep and the barbed innuendo arrowed into His spirit.

His critics were quick to pounce on the fact that He had not been properly trained as a rabbi, been suitably educated or been to the right rabbinic schools (John 7:15).

He was ridiculed for His Messianic pretensions. Only stupid people would follow a mere man – what did they know? (John 7:49).

He was reviled for His *modus operandi* – instead of fawning on the rich and courting the powerful He befriended sinners (Matt. 11:19). He was stereotyped and categorised to keep Him controllable. He was typecast by religious leaders as a Messiah created in their own image and then cold-shouldered when He did not fit in with their self-serving agenda.

From early in His ministry He had been threatened. He passed through an angry crowd as if breaching a hostile picket line (Luke 4:30). He was repeatedly harassed and led a fast-moving, almost fugitive, existence as His enemies sought occasion to arrest Him.

Finally cornered, He was 'looked after by the secret police'. Made sport of, mocked, subjected to sleep-deprived interrogation, He was bullied and abused.

All this and more is evoked by Peter's words which tear off the page like a firsthand account. You can almost hear the hate-filled haranguing of a humiliated and pain-wracked victim. The insults which add to the injury are a further indictment of man's inhumanity to man. The physical brutality is matched by the verbal vilification.

Remarkably and savingly, Jesus absorbs the poison of hate. His self-giving love is the effective antidote to the self-destructive cruelty of sin. He does not return insult for insult. The vile threats are left hanging in the humid air to shame the critics. He returns forgiveness for ferocity, trust for betrayal. He revokes the law of retaliation, He breaks the cycle of violence.

Violence has its ultimate victim, God's own Son, and fails to win. The last scapegoat perishes in the arid desert.

The demeanour of the dying Jesus evokes Isaiah's moving portrait of the benign reactions of God's Suffering Servant under extreme duress. His agony is compounded by His own innocence: 'He committed no sin, and no deceit was found in his mouth' (2:22; Isa. 53:9).

His whole life to this moment has been one of faithful obedience, and at the last He 'entrusted himself to him who judges justly' (2:23). Handed over by His accusers to the Roman soldiers for ill-treatment, He – in sovereign freedom – hands Himself over to God's keeping. He models the divine reaction for us (cf 4:19), handing over to God both Himself for vindication and His enemies for judgment.

2:24a The cross *removes the burden of sin*
'He himself bore our sins ...'

So far, Peter has had one eye on the suffering Christ and one eye on the pressure his readers are facing, notably those who were slaves in first-century households (2:18). But the more he surveys the wondrous cross the more deeply he sees not only a pattern of enduring pain that will stiffen the resistance of his oppressed readers – what concerns *you* – but its larger and atoning meaning which concerns all of *us*.

The cross represents the extent of God's loving intention to plunge deeper and deeper into our world. That saving mercy reaches further and further down, first into our humanity, and then, in our humanity, into our moral struggles and human suffering, and reaches its furthest limit by entering into our alienation and abandonment and takes it upon itself.

However terrible the agony of Jesus in His sufferings and death, it was not only a passion but an achievement. Of that the apostles are sure. Looking at the awful sight of the tortured Saviour nailed to the cursed tree, we may properly be so occupied with what He is enduring that we are oblivious to what He is accomplishing. But Peter sees something remarkable occurring through the agony inflicted on Jesus.

An astonishing exchange, a strangely wonderful substitution, is going on. Jesus, in dying, takes our place, stands in for us, assumes our responsibilities as sin had fixed them, pays the wages due to us sinners, discharges the debt we owed, makes our obligations His own, avenges our enemies, pays the ransom that frees us. No wonder John Bunyan's Pilgrim leapt to find his burden had rolled away!

2:24b The cross *renews our life*
'… that we might die to sins and live for righteousness …'

If the sublime atonement theology which assures us that 'he himself bore our sins' is ever misused, it is in inducing a complacency that makes us again spectators of the crucifixion. We go wrong if we simply assume that Jesus does all the dying and we do all the living. In theologians' language, there is no substitution ('he himself bore our sins') without identification ('so that we might die to sins …').

Sin viewed in these terms is a power whose hold on us is broken only by a kind of dying. When we meet Jesus in His death we are drawn into that death for sin with Him. Thus in His death we die to the power of sin, in His self-surrender our self-defeat is spelt out. Only by going down into death *with Him* do we rise up with Him to share His new life.

To change the metaphor, we need healing and restoration to health. We live in a world made sick by sin. Salvation is for us a recovery of spiritual health. And this is what the cross achieves.

'By his wounds you have been healed' (2:24c). Only wounds heal wounds. Grafting takes place in horticulture when the open wound of one plant is joined to the open wound of another. So the wound of God is set close to the wound of the world to rejuvenate a sick creation and to renew its life. T.S. Eliot captured this paradox memorably in his image of the 'wounded surgeon':

> Beneath the bleeding hands, we feel
> The sharp compassion of the healer's art …[64]

Echoing Eliot, Peter Kreeft writes, 'We needed a surgeon, and he came and reached into our wounds with bloody hands. He didn't give us a placebo or a pill or good advice. He gave us himself.'[65]

2:25 The cross *restores our relationship with God*
'… but now you have returned to the Shepherd and Overseer of your souls.'

Just beneath the surface of these words is Isaiah's graphic metaphor for wayward people – that of straying sheep losing their way – made even more vivid in the parable of Jesus about the reach and intensity of His own shepherding ministry that sought the least, the last and the lost.

And this picture in turn tells the larger story recounted throughout Scripture of universal human alienation and estrangement due to sin. Sin in these terms is *relational*. Sin is deviance.

But the Good Shepherd stays relentless in His pursuing love, descending into the deep abyss into which we had fallen. The Overseer never loses sight of even the most determined prodigal in the furthest country of his self-imposed exile.

In salvation we are reconciled to our suffering, seeking Creator. We are drawn back to the holy heart that predates our fall and even our creation (cf 1:19b). We are returned home.

I remember singing as a young boy an old revivalist hymn:

I must needs go home by the way of the cross,
There's no other way but this;
I shall ne'er get sight of the Gates of Light,
If the way of the cross I miss.

Jürgen Moltmann, in reflecting on Luther's famous dictum *crux probia omnia*, reminds us that 'the cross is the test of everything which deserves to be called Christian'.[66]

The cross is the prism through which are refracted all the rainbow colours of salvation.

The way forward is the way of the cross.

The way for us is His way too.

The way down is the way up.

The way through is the way out.

The way of the cross leads home.

James Denney, Scottish Presbyterian that he was, spoke once of those Christians who minimise the importance of the cross and was glad to admit, 'If I had the choice between being such a person or a Roman Catholic priest, I had rather be the priest lifting up the crucifix to a dying man, and saying, "God loves like that!"'[67]

Prayer and Reflection

Lord, we accept we are different.
   We accept this not as a handicap to be overcome
   but as a gift to be exploited.

Lord, You know that in our oddness we are liable to be
   ostracised by those fearful of us,
   patronised by the superior,
   marginalised by the more powerful.
Lord, we accept this, too, as the cost of following Jesus, and only
ask that You will give us His Spirit of self-restraint and non-
retaliation.

Lord, You know we can feel isolated and lonely 'in the land of
forgetfulness'.
Remember us
   in the hospital bed,
   in the staff canteen,
   in the company boardroom,
   in the sports club.

When anonymity threatens to overwhelm us ...
Good Shepherd, remind us that You know us and call us by name;
Great Overseer, reassure us You never lose sight of us.

Give us the courage to express our strangeness
   in strange new acts of goodness,
   in unlikely loving and unexpected kindness,
   in surprising forgiveness and startling mercy,
   in odd uses of our freedom to serve others.

In the strong name of our sin-bearing Saviour in whose footsteps
we follow.
Amen.

- Reflect on the wisdom we need to be *holy*-different without becoming holier-than-thou!
- Think of creative ways in which we might surprise the world with expressions of God's love.

GOD'S PEOPLE THINK DIFFERENTLY ABOUT THE GOOD LIFE

1 PETER

3:1-7 Sharing the good life – as spouses

Wives and Husbands

[1]Wives, in the same way be submissive to your husbands so that, if any of them do not believe the word, they may be won over without words by the behaviour of their wives, [2]when they see the purity and reverence of your lives. [3]Your beauty should not come from outward adornment, such as braided hair and the wearing of gold jewellery and fine clothes. [4]Instead, it should be that of your inner self, the unfading beauty of a gentle and quiet spirit, which is of great worth in God's sight. [5]For this is the way the holy women of the past who put their hope in God used to make themselves beautiful. They were submissive to their own husbands, [6]like Sarah, who obeyed Abraham and called him her master. You are her daughters if you do what is right and do not give way to fear.

[7]Husbands, in the same way be considerate as you live with your wives, and treat them with respect as the weaker partner and as heirs with you of the gracious gift of life, so that nothing will hinder your prayers.

'Submission' sparks with contention in our modern world. Since Islam, we recall, basically means 'submission', we may say that half the world dreads it, while half the world is in thrall to it.

There can scarcely be a more reviled concept in the modern Western Church than 'submission', in particular the submission of women to men! And not without good reason.

Peter's words – and others like them in the New Testament – are rejected either as being inherently oppressive or as being hopelessly traditional and therefore outmoded.

Firstly, no one can doubt that these texts have a bitter history, having been misused to oppress and even abuse women.

In Canadian novelist Margaret Attwood's horrific fantasy, *The Handmaid's Tale*, words such as Peter's transmute into 'texts of terror'. The novel is set in the futuristic Republic of Gilead where women's freedoms have been severely curtailed by a patriarchal totalitarianism. Lesser women are drones, set to do menial work. More presentable women are housed in special breeding centres in order to 'serve' the leaders and produce pure stock for the society. Women are secure, safe on the streets, sufficiently provided for, but are effectively slaves! In bitter irony, Scripture passages such as 1 Peter 3 and the Sermon on the Mount are read out while all this goes on!

Aunt Lydia, spin doctor for the regime, tries to sustain the lie by reassuring the surrogate mother at the centre of the tale, whom we know only by her designated name 'Offred', that 'There is more than one kind of freedom … Freedom to and freedom from. In the days of anarchy, it was freedom to. Now you are being given freedom from. Don't underrate it.'[68]

Before we dismiss Attwood's vision as feminist polemic, it is worth hearing the salutary note it strikes. No ideology is more tragic than one which is a power-driven distortion of the truth. No system is more dangerous than one which believes itself to have uncritical divine support. The evil one himself, we know, can bolster his case with scriptural quotations. Fortunately evil does not have the last word on exegesis!

Secondly, it is true that texts like this are cast in a 'traditional' mould. In line with the other apostles, Peter here concurs with the usual Christian adaptation of the traditional 'household code'. This is sometimes unfairly criticised as if the newness of the gospel precludes honouring the wisdom of the past or necessitates novelty at every turn.

We are certainly redeemed *from* futile inherited ways but that does not mean that *everything* in pre-Christian society was wrong. In fact as G.K. Chesterton observed, it is only Christianity which, while repudiating idolatry, preserves the best in paganism 'because it is only Christian men who guard heathen things'.[69]

Christians themselves differ over whether the exhortation means 'willingly submit to authority and leadership' or whether it has a softer meaning of 'defer, honour, and respect the order of the day' as perhaps the context demands.[70]

My brief comments will not settle this issue but a number of reflections may be made:

1) Christlikeness is being invoked. The subordination Jesus showed was not inferiority; although He was equal with His Father He chose voluntarily to submit.

It is not enough to remember old texts; they can be tragically misused. It is all the more vital to *remember Jesus*.[71]

If there is a 'balm in Gilead' it can only be the Christ whose self-giving, suffering love we are called to emulate.

Holy law, Islamic or otherwise, may subdue the world; only holy love will save it!

2) Radical moves are afoot in giving those deemed at the time to be inferior the dignity and freedom to act as responsible moral agents.

The words are addressed not to husbands but to wives, and no husband should be misled into exploiting this text to tell his wife to submit to him.

If this was subordination, it was – as John Yoder pointed out – a '*revolutionary* subordination'.

3) Tactical considerations are in operation to do with evangelism. Here, with unbelieving husbands, it can be a subtle and effective means of witness so that unbelieving husbands may be 'won without words'. In such tense situations, a believing wife's daring act of faith (cf Sarah, 3:6) can free her from fear.

4) Deep attitudes, not superficial appearances, are being addressed. What is most important is what a woman is on the inside (3:3ff.). What is her 'spiritual make-up'? Exposing what is inward rather than outward (vv.3–4a) shows if beauty is only skin deep.

Now, these verses should not be heard as condemning Christian women for being well dressed or looking attractive. Who does not despise the stereotypical view of Christian women as drab and dowdy? But the passage is probing what lies behind the mask because this is what is most important. God offers the spiritual jewellery of a 'gentle and quiet spirit'.

All this is aimed at turning our lives Godward rather than manward (3:4c).

The honour issue surfaces again – what is God's valuation of worth? Women particularly are encouraged to dress and behave not with the sole aim of attracting men all the time but of pleasing God! The word 'adornment' in verse 3 is *kosmos* from which we derive the word 'cosmetic'.

A glimpse into its first-century context may help us hear this passage better. Bruce Winter quotes the historian T.A.J. McGinn to the effect that 'in classical antiquity you were what you wore'.[72] Winter points out that around 44 BC a 'new' type of Roman woman began to emerge who demanded more sexual freedom, asserted the right to choose her lovers, and also called for more financial independence.

In such a context the removal of the traditional veil, for example, would have signalled, if not prostitution, at least the sexual 'come on' of the permissive 'new' Roman woman. Critics of the new Christian movement, Winter suggests, seeing Christian wives 'dressed to kill', might well have concluded that 'they belonged to a promiscuous cult that endorsed *avant-guarde* behaviour'.[73]

Fashion codes come and go. Peter's wise words can be updated for every age and generation. What is at issue is how free we are from the fads and pressures of a consumer society which has a vested interest in obsolescence. Christians are not called to put lip-gloss on the world.

Even the most vivacious young Christian woman today might hear these verses as a gracious call to godly freedom and so might avoid turning heads merely because of the 'dress she's almost wearing'!

If whatever in the past is redeemable by grace then surely whatever in the *present* is pure, lovely and praiseworthy is redeemable also. Might a Christian be a fashion model? In today's climate, I doubt the wisdom of it. But why not more dress designers, makers of jewellery, and artists of all kinds? Scripture here is not out to cramp anyone's style but to prophetically challenge our conformity to the celebrity-obsessed and image-conscious age in which we live (cf 1 Sam. 16:7).[74]

3:7

For his part the husband likewise must recognise that his wife is:

- almost certainly physically weaker (or sometimes emotionally more vulnerable), and
- *spiritually equal in every respect.*

With this in mind, he is urged to 'live considerately' or 'according to knowledge'. Such considerateness may, in the words of Wayne Grudem, be expected to 'include any knowledge that would be beneficial to the husband-wife relationship; knowledge of God's purposes and principles for marriage; knowledge of the wife's desires, goals, and frustrations; knowledge of her strengths and weaknesses in the physical, emotional and spiritual realms. A husband who lives according to such knowledge will greatly enrich his marriage relationship.'[75]

Above all, the Christian husband, if he is to sustain a prayerful rapport with God, must honour his wife as a full spiritual equal as, in Peter's lovely phrase, *joint heirs of God's gracious gift of life.* I see no reason to confine the meaning of this lovely phrase to the sharing of only spiritual or eternal life, precious and enriching as that is. Just a year or two before he died, that much-loved veteran teacher of the Church, Lewis Smedes, reflected on this:

As I have slowly crept into decrepitude, I have been surprised at how often I feel washed in warm waves of awe at the graces of life. They come over me when my wife and I sit down to supper and we start counting the blessings we have been given that day. The deeper my wonder at the gift of a day almost gone, the stronger my hope becomes for the one on the way. And the brighter my memory of the gifts of good days, the stronger may be my hope in the dark days on the way.[76]

Because Jesus humbled Himself and stooped to wash dirty feet, we can retain our human dignity and equality before God without having always to assert our rights.

Because Jesus was victimised for us on the cross, no one, least of all women, should be expected to bear unjust abuse, and certainly not in the name of submission.

Because Jesus lives in resurrection reality, we can be sure that the way things are now is not the way things will be in God's future.

Because Jesus is Lord, we are free to call anyone else 'lord' only in a relative and highly minimalist sense and should refuse to do so in any case where that impinges on His sole sovereignty over our lives.

As Allen Verhey concedes, the New Testament words on this matter are all *male* words but, he reminds us, they are spoken by men who, 'faithful to the memory of Jesus, have broken the Gileads within and challenged and qualified the Gileads without'. If we react against these words and unthinkingly reject them we lose touch with the critical memory of Jesus and miss the potential in these words for radical social change. But 'if we use these words to silence women and to mute their voices ... we will be serving Gilead, not the alternative future Christ proclaimed and whose power he made known'.[77]

One final, personal thought. In my experience, where true Christian love, genuine respect and mutual trust exist in a marriage, one never hears the matter of submission raised at all!

Leonard Cheshire was Britain's leading bomber ace of the Second World War. He was an official observer who flew with the US raid which dropped the atom bomb on Hiroshima.

After the war, becoming a devout Catholic, he met and married Sue Ryder, and together they devoted themselves to caring for the disabled, for leper victims, and for the terminally ill for the rest of their lives. The night before their wedding in Bombay they composed this prayer:

Thou, O my God,
Who art infinite love,
Yet who has called us to be perfect
Even as Thou art perfect,
Who so loved the world
That Thou hast given us Thine only begotten Son
And hast thereby given us Thine all, Thine everything,
Who emptied Thyself of Thy glory,
And was made obedient unto death,
Even the death of the Cross
For us.
To Thee
We offer our all, our everything,
To be consumed in the unquenchable fire of Thy love.
We desire to love Thee even as Thy own Mother loved Thee,
To be generous as Thou Thyself was generous,
To give our all to Thee even as Thou hast given Thine to us.
Thou hast called us, O Lord, and we have found Thee,
In the sick, the unwanted and the dying,
And there we will serve Thee
Unto death.[78]

As in many areas of life, so, it seems, with this: starting well is all-important.

3:8–12 Sharing the good life – as brothers and sisters

Suffering for Doing Good

⁸Finally, all of you, live in harmony with one another; be sympathetic, love as brothers, be compassionate and humble. ⁹Do not repay evil with evil or insult with insult, but with blessing, because to this you were called so that you may inherit a blessing. ¹⁰For,

'Whoever would love life
    and see good days
must keep his tongue from evil
    and his lips from deceitful speech.
¹¹He must turn from evil and do good;
    he must seek peace and pursue it.
¹²For the eyes of the Lord are on the righteous
    and his ears are attentive to their prayer,
but the face of the Lord is against those who do evil.'

The Good Life remains, over thirty years after it was made, one of Britain's best-loved classic TV sit-coms which still gets regular airings. In this the 'Goods' – Tom and Barbara (wonderfully played by Richard Briers and Felicity Kendall) – turn their backs on the commuter rat-race and dig up their suburban garden in an effort to become self-sufficient. Much of the humour stems from their interaction with their posh and snobbish neighbour, Margo Leadbetter (Penelope Keith), and her long-suffering businessman husband, Jerry (the late Paul Eddington), over what constitutes the 'good life' in the clash of lifestyles.

But in these verses the 'good life' is not being defined as either the materialistic consumerism or the whimsical escapism offered so wittily as options by the comedy. Peter stakes out a claim for a truly alternative society.

The righteous life spoken of here is surely a fruit of the cross, flowing from our believing identification with Jesus in His death (cf 2:24).

First, it involves *right relationships* (3:8). Righteousness, in the Old Testament's vision, is primarily a term describing right relation to, or integrity to, an agreed covenantal relationship. The revelation of God through Christ and the Spirit as love-in-Trinity confirms for us that the essence of ultimate reality is relational.

Contrary to modern reports, the good life does not consist of self-assertion or acquisitiveness as defined by the advertising industry or the colour supplements!

So a fulfilled life is lived in harmony with one another. It is characterised by unity, sympathy, fellow-feeling, compassion and humility.

Second, it involves *right reactions* (3:9). The moving image of the non-retaliatory Jesus, painted for us in 2:21–23, comes flooding back into view. To give bitterness is to get bitterness back, but to give blessing is to receive blessing. No one spoke more wisely on this than the earlier sages of Israel, here represented by the quotation from Psalm 34. Their words could be bettered only when their vision of the truly human life stepped out of the text and was enfleshed in Jesus.

Here is a vision of life together which breaks through class barriers and social snobbery and dissolves rugged independence into humble and compassionate openness. The aggressive competitiveness of the winner-takes-all is driven out of business dealings and left to the sports field. And think how the political process might be startlingly transformed if we stopped trading insult for insult!

'Blessing' here involves loving life – in sharp contrast to those many sad souls who end up hating life.

It means to 'see good days' – not simply the good *old* days.

It means 'finding peace' and having 'the eyes of the Lord on you' and 'His ears open to your prayers'. This is life lived out in community under the favour of God and before the face of God. But there is a price to be paid for such a counter-cultural vision.

Prayer and Reflection

Lord, Your vision of the good life eclipses any other.
You offer us a genuine alternative:
    not escaping reality,
    not acquiring things,
    not lifestyle change or choice,
    not narcotic pleasure-seeking.
Decisively, we have been spoiled for lesser things;
Deeply and satisfyingly, we have 'tasted the goodness of the Lord'.

Lord, You bless us with long good days.
You alone give us good reasons for marriage.
You alone instil in us good habits of the heart.

You are making us connoisseurs of Your rich goodness.
We sit at creation's high table with a feast spread before us.
We sample Your fare at every turn:
    in music and mountains, in books and babies,
    in all beautiful things.
We sip the fine wine of Your grace wherever we find it.
We cup to our mouths the fresh water from a thousand delightful
streams – all traceable to You, the fountain of life.

Should suffering cloud this vision – as surely it will – unbidden and
often unjust …
May we taste Your goodness even then;
under pressure,
in pain,
may we find the grace to glorify You still.
By the 'good grief' of that first Easter make it so, we pray.
Amen.

- Make a list of all the things which most people deem are essential for a high standard of living and compare them with the example and teaching of Jesus.
- Dig out and share with one another the stories of the saints and martyrs and 'ordinary' Christians who have glorified God in suffering.

GOD'S PEOPLE REACT DIFFERENTLY TO PRESSURE

3:13-14   Suffering bravely

3:15-17   Sanctifying Christ as Lord

3:18-22   Secure in Christ's achievement
by His dying He restores us to our
rightful place:
the presence of God
by His rising He resumes His
rightful place:
the right hand of God
by His ascension He relegates the
forces of evil to their rightful place:
beneath His feet

4:1-6   Surprising the godless

1 PETER

3:13–14 Suffering bravely

[13]Who is going to harm you if you are eager to do good? [14]But even if you should suffer for what is right, you are blessed. Do not fear what they fear; do not be frightened.

How radically different this vision of human life is. The good life and blessing and suffering are all woven into the same fabric!

But this is not suffering for crimes committed or wrongs done; this is the blessing of *suffering for righteousness' sake* (cf Matt. 5:10). What definition of the good life currently on offer is going to include being willing to suffer for it?

Peter insists on the practicality of such a good life even amidst pressure and exhorts his readers to live in the 'good' of it.

3:14 'Don't fear what they fear'

This marks Christians out as different from those around them. We are not immune from the pressures and anxieties others face; in fact they are compounded by the hope-filled vision we have. But, empowered by the Spirit, we may react differently.

'Don't be afraid' stands out as the exhortation given most frequently in the Bible, and Peter is not above repeating it. Don't panic or respond neurotically to the world's fears.

Significantly, Peter quotes directly from Isaiah 8:12 which describes the remnant of disciples entrusted with the vision of the coming Messianic kingdom. Our conviction that God's kingdom *has come in measure and in advance* in Jesus emboldens us to overcome our fear. We refuse to be intimidated by the overbearing presence of whatever 'empire' we happen to be living in.

3:15–17 Sanctifying Christ as Lord

[15]But in your hearts set apart Christ as Lord. Always be prepared to give an answer to everyone who asks you to give the reason for the hope that you have. But do this with gentleness and respect, [16]keeping a clear conscience, so that those who speak maliciously against your good behaviour in Christ may be ashamed of their slander. [17]It is better, if it is God's will, to suffer for doing good than for doing evil.

However little we may see of the glory of God's kingdom made public and visible in society, however hostile the forces that bear down on us, we can keep our inner space sacrosanct.

Each Christian heart is a throne room in which Christ presides as Lord. Focus on Him as Lord and filter out all other competing factors for control of your life at this point. This is the command centre of consecration or sanctification, as we see from the language Peter uses here ('in your hearts set apart Christ as Lord'). At the deepest core level of our personality we 'set Christ apart' as the supreme and sole authority over our whole being. Every public step of discipleship starts with this private act of devotion (cf Rom. 10:9).

As in Isaiah's prophetic oracle (Isa. 8:13), the Lord is the one we fear, and so we can withstand the pressure to conform from outside and take our orders only from Him. Nerved by this cast-iron inner conviction, notable Christians – from Martin Luther to Martin Luther King – have faced down their enemies and uttered their 'Here I stand. I can do no other.'

3:15b Be ready to give a defence to those who ask

Our 'apologia' is not an apology but is more akin to what we now call 'apologetics' – explaining the faith with reasoned answers. These are best given, in my experience, after, not before, people inquire. Too often the Church is answering questions the world isn't asking!

And notice that 'hope' again, as throughout this letter, is the key issue. We are not expected to have *all the answers* to every query others put to us. As believers in Jesus Christ, the first point of contact with unbelievers may simply raise the tentative inquiry as to why you and I are hopeful. What reason do we have for hope in such a despairing world?

And when we respond, says Peter, we are to do so with gentleness and 'respect'. We do not need to be defensive – we are not justifying ourselves. Nor are we attacking an opponent with 'our' truth. Instead we are offering a reason for the Christ-shaped, resurrection-based hope that has been given to us.

3:16 Keep a good conscience

This was fixed in baptism (3:21). We can thereafter act, react, speak and suffer with a clear conscience before God knowing that we are in His will (so verse 17) and that being in His will is best.

Any unjust suffering for the good life ultimately rests on the achievement of Jesus who Himself suffered unjustly – 'the righteous for the unrighteous' – but in doing so brought us to God, triumphed over death and declared His victory over every enemy and the devil. It is the achievement of the cross that nerves us to suffer unjustly in the cause of righteousness. And to this Peter now turns.

3:18–22 Secure in Christ's achievement

[18]For Christ died for sins once for all, the righteous for the unrighteous, to bring you to God. He was put to death in the body but made alive by the Spirit, [19]through whom also he went and preached to the spirits in prison [20]who disobeyed long ago when God waited patiently in the days of Noah while the ark was being built.

In it only a few people, eight in all, were saved through water, [21]and this water symbolises baptism that now saves you also – not the removal of dirt from the body but the pledge of a good conscience towards God. It saves you by the resurrection of Jesus Christ, [22]who has gone into heaven and is at God's right hand – with angels, authorities and powers in submission to him.

In these words Peter is following a clear sequence of thought, though he does diverge significantly at one point.

Christ suffered for our sins, once-for-all (*hapax*).

He was put to death in the flesh ...

He was made alive in spirit/or 'by the Spirit' (the consensus view is that this refers to Christ's resurrection) through which (or 'through whom' or 'in which') He went ('having gone', as in verse 22, to heaven) 'to the spirits in prison who disobeyed long ago when God waited patiently in the days of Noah ...'

At the mention of Noah, Peter then goes off at a tangent, returning to the main story-line in verse 22, speaking of Christ 'who has gone into heaven and is at God's right hand – with angels, authorities and powers in submission to him'.

Let's outline the dramatic story of salvation summarised here:

1) By His dying He restores us to our rightful place: the presence of God.
2) By His rising He resumes His rightful place: the right hand of God.
3) By His ascension He relegates the forces of evil to their rightful place: beneath His feet.

1) *By His dying He restores us to our rightful place: the presence of God*
There are four special points of profound interest here:

First, He 'died for sins'. His death, as we have been reminded at 2:24, was not a random killing or tragic accident. His was a death with real atoning value. It deals with the problem caused by our sins as nothing else can.

Second, He died, 'the righteous for the unrighteous'. This is the amazing saving action of the One who stands in for us, who takes our place of condemnation and bears all our sins away (cf 2:24). His was an atoning death. There's nothing more bitter than innocent or unjust suffering.

What it might have meant to a pure and unsinning soul like Christ's to come into such close contact with sin we cannot imagine. Even less can we know the horror of bearing the full weight of official condemnation and unofficial hatred by One who was wholly innocent of any charges made against Him.

Third, He died 'once for all'. The word *hapax* signifies something that is unique and unrepeated, a point of which the writer to the Hebrews makes much (Heb. 9:25–28; 10:10–12).

Fourth, He died 'to bring you to God'. Removing the sin which was a barrier to fellowship with God, He 'brings us to God'.

Every religion in the world claims to have some handle on this, claims a facility in connecting people with God. We must be careful not to denigrate other world religions, but the Old Testament prophets and New Testament apostles are as one in viewing the idolatrous religious systems of the ancient world as 'futile exercises' (1:18). However zealously practised, they remain unable to bring the worshipper into effective contact with God. (Not even Judaism did this, as Hebrews explains.)

But by His atoning death, Jesus 'brings us to God' and effects reconciliation with Him. The particular word Peter uses (*prosago*) is vivid and instructive and drawn from Roman court imagery. It described the work of an offical whose job it was to admit people to an audience with a great king or dignitary. So Jesus, in His death as our sponsor, introduces us to the very presence of a holy God.

Paul, too, employs this same image in Romans 5:2 where he says that we have been given 'access' to the grace in which we stand. In Ephesians 2:18 he says that through Christ both Jew and Gentile have 'access' to the Father.

In James Denney's view, 'The word always has a touch of formality in it; it is a great occasion when the Son who has assumed our responsibilities for us takes us by the hand to bring us to the Father.'[79]

Every approach to God in prayer or worship, resting as it does on His shed blood, was and is a great honour invested with awe and majesty and wonder.

2) By His rising He resumes His rightful place: the right hand of God
'He was put to death in the body but made alive by the Spirit' (3:18). This seems at first glance like the normal way of telling the story of Christ's death and resurrection – and I think it is.

But what blurs the picture and opens the door in some people's eyes to an unprecedented interpretation of the next verse is the Greek word used here. It is the word *zoopoiethis* and it is used nowhere else in the New Testament for the resurrection. Add to it the phrase 'by the Spirit' or 'in the spirit' and the way is open for those who want to force a distinction between 'being made alive in the spirit' and 'the resurrection' which is mentioned in verse 21.

On this line of interpretation, while Jesus' body remained in the tomb, His 'spirit' was quickened to life and became active.

This is almost certainly a wrong conclusion to draw. There is evidence from the Greek Old Testament (the Septuagint) of the two terms for death and aliveness being used together (2 Kings 5:7, Septuagint).

A further consideration here is that the three main verbs applying to Jesus in this section all have passive participle endings – *theis* – suggesting that they form a consecutive sequence and confirming our line of thought.

- *thanatotheis* – 'having been put to death' (3:18)
- *zoopoiethis* – 'having been made alive' (3:18)
- *poreutheis* – 'having gone into heaven' (3:22)

This strongly implies that Peter did not have in mind any deviation from the normal sequence of events.

And what of 'in the body' and 'in' or 'by spirit'? The overwhelming consensus in biblical scholarship is that the distinction is *not* between a material and an immaterial part of Christ's Person (ie His body and soul). Rather, the distinction is between *two spheres of existence.* On the one hand is His earthly existence, subject to human limitations; on the other is the sphere of Christ's existence in which God's Spirit was supremely and conspicuously at work – namely His resurrection state of power, vindication and new life (cf Rom. 1:3; 1 Tim. 3:16). This distinction is exactly what applies in 4:6. Ramsey Michaels writes:

> The statement that Christ was 'made alive in the spirit' therefore means simply that he was raised from the dead, not as a spirit, but bodily (as resurrection always was in the New Testament) and in a sphere in which the Spirit and power of God are displayed without hindrance or human limitation.[80]

Peter Davids agrees and says:

> [Christ died] with respect to flesh. But he died as a whole person not simply as a body. Christ was made alive (and note the *made* alive for here as usual the action of the Father in raising him from the dead is assumed) ... in respect to the spirit, the mode of existence of the regenerate and those who please God ...

Davids continues:

> It was not that the spirit or soul of Christ was dead and that it alone was made alive, nor that Christ took leave of the flesh. But that in the resurrection life of his whole person, body as well as spirit, he took leave of further identification with sin and thus of the further need to die (he suffered 'once'); he now lives as a resurrected

person in the mode of existence in which Christians, even before resurrection, can participate, body and soul, although their complete participation awaits the redemption of the body.[81]

Raised to life again, it was impossible any longer for death to hold Him.

Re-entering heaven itself (3:22) by the strangest miracle of all – the ascension.

Regaining His rightful place, He is reinstated – at God's right hand! There He exercises power and authority in the spiritual realm over all the forces of evil now subject to Him.

The clear implication is that the proclamation to the spirits takes place *after*, not before, His resurrection. Let's look at this more closely.

3) *By His ascension He relegates the forces of evil to their rightful place: beneath His feet*

Chapter 3 verse 19 is the contentious verse which our previous discussion has gone a long way to resolve. On this verse have been built clauses in the creed – 'He descended into hell' – and, in both medieval art and in some popular preaching circles, elaborate and dramatic reconstructions of the dead Christ 'harrowing hell'.

Three main views have been forwarded:

First, Christ came to the place where *disobedient supernatural powers* ('spirits') have been imprisoned since the days of Noah.

He did this by a journey either *downwards* – as it were – to *Hades* and *before His resurrection*, or *upwards* – as it were – to *heaven* and *after His resurrection*.

He went to proclaim His victory over them as part of His heavenly exaltation (3:22) that shows Him now to be superior to all powers (3:22).

Second, Christ went to *Hades* to preach to the *spirits of people who were disobedient in Noah's day.*

He went to proclaim either *victory and judgment* or *the gospel,*

126

offering them – as it were – *a second chance* after death! (Some have suggested this at least for the generation destroyed in the Flood.)

Third, Christ, by the power of the Spirit of God, *entered into Noah* when he – that is, Noah – preached righteousness to the disobedient generation of his day. (Augustine taught this; Wayne Grudem argues for this today.)

What are we to make of it? Howard Marshall has a very helpful discussion of this matter within the framework of four questions.[82]

Of Christ's proclamation to the spirits in prison we may ask:

First, when did He go? On Grudem's view, Christ preached in and through Noah by the Spirit. Perhaps 1:10 bears on this. See also 2 Peter 2:5. But 'made alive', as we saw above, much more naturally fits the sequence of Christ's Easter and ascension victory over death – resurrection and ascent to heaven. So it is very likely that no backward reference is here intended.

So it is better to say that *He performed the task in the realm of the Spirit before going to heaven.*

However, there are still two options:

- He went between Good Friday and Easter Day. He descended into Hades, the temporary abode of the dead (but definitely not hell), where the disobedient spirits are imprisoned.
- He went after His resurrection, visiting the spirits during His ascension in their traditional abode of the 'heavenly realms'.

Second, where did He go? In line with the first option above, He went to the abode of the dead (*Sheol* in the Old Testament; Psa. 30:3; Isa. 14:15; Matt. 12:40; Acts 2:27,31).

On this view Christ's spirit was active when separated from His still-dead body.

In line with the second option above is the Jewish belief in several 'levels' or 'layers' in heaven. See Paul's 'third heaven' (2 Cor. 12:2). Some Jewish thinkers located the place where evil powers are kept in subjection until judgment in one of these levels.

On this view there is no need, and it is wrong, to separate Christ's soul from His body in His 'being made alive'.

Third, to whom did Christ go? What does 'spirits' refer to?

One view is that *'spirits' are the spirits of dead people in the abode of the dead.* But the word is only once used like this in the New Testament in Hebrews 12:23.

This difficulty faces the view of Christ preaching in Noah's time also.

Describing the spirits as 'disobedient' perhaps fits the Genesis narrative in which only eight were saved (Gen. 8:18). But the eight are described not as 'spirits' but as *psychai* ('eight persons', 3:20, NRSV).

And in what sense was God waiting patiently for them to repent?

It is also unprecedented for the spirits of the dead to be regarded as held in prison.

A second view is that *'spirits' are evil, supernatural beings.* The term is often used of angels and evil beings (Heb. 1:14; 12:9 – not 'our spirits' as in the NIV; Acts 23:8–9; and Mark 1:23; Luke 10:20; Acts 19:15–16).

Furthermore the Genesis 6 story was popular in New Testament times (cf 1 Enoch and 2 Peter 2:4; Jude 6).

The second view is the least difficult and corresponds to 3:22.

Fourth, what did He preach? Advocates of the views that Christ preached through Noah or to evil spirits before His resurrection usually answer this question, in one way or another, by saying that *He preached the gospel.* Some claim this was with a view to the audience being saved.

But it is more likely that *kerusso* is being used in its standard sense of 'proclaim' or 'declare as a herald'. If this is the case it is probable that *Christ's proclamation to the evil powers is an announcement of*

His total victory over them on the cross confirming their defeat.

Peter shares this conviction with Paul (Col. 2:15; Eph. 1:22).

If this is the correct interpretation of this difficult passage – as I believe it is – then Peter is reassuring his readers that *whatever evil they are facing, they must stand up to it in the strength of the Christ who by His death and resurrection has utterly routed the forces of evil and now rules over them in triumph.*

So verses 21 and 23 draw together the three parties in this cosmic drama:

- Ourselves – the objects of His saving mission, saved through His resurrection
- Jesus Christ – in so far as He acts for God and is now 'at God's right hand'
- Evil powers – decisively overcome and now 'in submission to him'.

To the question 'How do we appropriate Christ's victory?' the answer given here is *through faith-baptism* (3:20b–22).[83]

It is significant that our best analogy for baptism is not the sprinkling that dampens but the flood that drowns! Noah's deliverance through water prefigures Christian baptism. As Noah found grace by committing himself to the ark and was brought safely through the flood waters of judgment and death so we, by entrusting ourselves in faith to the Christ who died and rose for us, are brought through the 'flood' of death and judgment on sin and are saved. Analogous to Noah, we step over into the whole new world of God's new creation.

Peter makes it clear that there is no magical quality in the water that achieves this. This is not to say that baptism is mere symbolism. Baptism actually saves us, though as the focused enactment of the engagement in the drama of both faith and divine action. Central to the act is the 'pledge' made by the believer which proceeds from a conscience made clean by the atoning death of Jesus. Most likely, the pledge is 'given in response to a demand: the baptismal candidate answers affirmatively to God's request for faith and obedience'.[84] This perhaps took place in a question-and-answer, catechetical dialogue between baptiser and baptised, an exchange hinted at in Acts 8 and more fully developed in the Early Church.

The seriousness of the commitment being made in baptism is reflected by the use made of the term 'pledge' for the sealing of a contract or a soldier's oath of allegiance.

The saving efficacy in baptism derives directly and entirely from the achievement of Jesus ('by the resurrection of Jesus Christ', 3:21c). Jesus is our 'ark of salvation' who has died for our sins to bring us to God, has been raised from the dead, has triumphed over evil, and has gone into heaven itself to sit at God's majestic right hand (3:22). Faith in Him enacted in baptism brings us through the waters of death into the whole new realm of reality which is His new creation (cf 1:3).

Peter thus bolsters the resistance of his baptised readers. In George Beasley-Murray's words, 'No power therefore can assail the Christian baptised in his name. The victory of Christ is complete and assures us of our part in the final redemption when we, too, shall know resurrection from God.'[85]

This is truly tough grace and living hope.

Since Christians are baptised by faith into God's new creation and born again to a living hope by Christ's resurrection how could the future not look different to us?

4:1-6 Surprising the godless

[1]Therefore, since Christ suffered in his body, arm yourselves also with the same attitude, because he who has suffered in his body is done with sin. [2]As a result, he does not live the rest of his earthly life for evil human desires, but rather for the will of God. [3]For you have spent enough time in the past doing what pagans choose to do – living in

debauchery, lust, drunkenness, orgies, carousing and detestable idolatry. ⁴They think it strange that you do not plunge with them into the same flood of dissipation, and they heap abuse on you. ⁵But they will have to give account to him who is ready to judge the living and the dead. ⁶For this is the reason the gospel was preached even to those who are now dead, so that they might be judged according to men in regard to the body, but live according to God in regard to the spirit.

Having left the past behind (4:3), Christians can look to and live for the future. Such a stance transforms 'the rest of his earthly life' (4:2).

Today is the first day of the rest of my life – what am I going to do with it? We should:

First, be willing to suffer for the sake of righteousness (cf 3:17). Peter exhorts his readers to 'arm yourselves' with Christ's 'attitude' (4:1). Be as resistant as He was to the claims of sin and to all that is not the will of God (even unto death). For this reason He suffered, resisting sin to the point of dying as the sin-bearer on the cross for us. So we are called to 'armed resistance' to sin in our lives.

Second, live the rest of our life for the will of God and not to satisfy our own will. Avoid compromise with the self-gratifying compulsions and addictions of the culture around us (4:2). Our motto should never be 'If it feels good do it' but 'What does He want me to be or do or say?' We must ask ourselves 'What pleases Him?' and 'What's in it for Him?' We may well surprise the godless by breaking with the idolatry of autonomous self-fulfilment pursued by our neighbours.

Third, be a non-conformist in the culture (4:3–4). Having broken with the past, live for the future. Pre-conversion time was more than long enough to do what pagans do. Now live as those newly born for God's future. Reforge the broken link between worship and ethics. Be aware how close is sensual sin to idolatrous behaviour.

Fourth, look to the judgment ahead and be accountable (4:5).

Pagans are accountable to no one but themselves. Most people in the modern world feel they can do or say anything they want – sometimes with the proviso 'as long as it hurts no one else'. Of course it's not always easy to predict the likely outcome for good or ill of one's own selfish behaviour, is it?

Fifth, expect vindication (4:6). Those Christians *now* physically dead had *previously* had the gospel preached to them. As a result, though judged and written off by human standards – by those who are of the 'flesh' – they can be sure in their resurrection life ('in regard to the spirit') of a favourable final verdict and an ultimate vindication which is modelled on His (cf 3:18–22).

Prayer and Reflection

Lord, we celebrate Your Easter victory,
We relish Your saving achievement,
We savour the old terms our fathers used to describe it:
    atonement – the just for the unjust,
    access – privileged introduction to the Holy of Holies,
    aliveness – Yours before ours, but Yours guaranteeing ours,
    ascension – Your vindication as God's righthand Man,
    authority – with all evil powers subject to You.
Hallelujah!

We thank You for our faith-baptism which brings us, like Noah, through the flood waters of judgment and death – to stand on new creation ground.

In the strength of Your victory
    we resist the conspiracy of fear all around us,
    we refuse to panic,
    we firmly but gently continue to give reasons for the hope
      You have given us.

Threatened by hostile forces wanting control of us
    we retreat to the command-centre deep in our hearts where
       Jesus reigns as Lord.
Armed with His authority and Spirit
    we surprise our neighbours by resisting the pagan pressure to join
       their plunge into sensuality.

Lord, give us the courage to stand up and be counted
and to let the difference show.
In Christ's name.
Amen.

- Read out loud to yourself or in a group – or even better sing –
  those old hymns and songs that tell the story of the wondrous
  cross and all it means for our salvation.
- Share with others the pressure you face at work or at home to
  lower your standards and live as the pagans do, and encourage
  one another to seek the victory that is yours in Christ.

GOD'S PEOPLE LOOK DIFFERENTLY AT THE FUTURE

4:7-11 Stewards of grace

> [7]The end of all things is near. Therefore be clear minded and self-controlled so that you can pray. [8]Above all, love each other deeply, because love covers over a multitude of sins. [9]Offer hospitality to one another without grumbling. [10]Each one should use whatever gift he has received to serve others, faithfully administering God's grace in its various forms. [11]If anyone speaks, he should do it as one speaking the very words of God. If anyone serves, he should do it with the strength God provides, so that in all things God may be praised through Jesus Christ. To him be the glory and the power for ever and ever. Amen.

A 'steward' – an *oikonomos* – was the term applied to a manager of a house or the administrator of an estate.

As applied to believers here two aspects surface.

1) *The attitudes of a steward*

First, a steward *lives for the future*. I often feel the whole eschatological bent of the Bible is exemplified by the fact that the Hebrew language is read from right to left!

Stewardship terminology is usually associated with the urgency demanded by the coming of God to call His people to account (cf Luke 12:42; 16:1–3). A steward is a person who lives and works in the light of the end or the final state of affairs. There is a future accountability that a steward cannot afford to avoid and a glory that a steward does not want to miss (cf 5:4,10). A wise steward sees that judgment for the Church has already begun (4:17).

The 'homeless' exiles have found a home in God's 'household'. However, it is not a place of cosy self-indulgence but the training ground for the new humanity.

Second, a steward *stays calm and self-controlled* (4:7). He doesn't lose his head (cf 5:8). He exercises sound judgment and displays a sober spirit (4:7). He has decided what to be serious about and what to sit lightly to and, because he has focused his emotional commitment, he does not dissipate his energy in all directions.

2) *The actions of a steward*

A good steward *keeps on loving* (4:8–9). Few words are more irrelevant than these – at least in the modern Western Church! They are irrelevant not because they are not practical and sharply applicable to our need but because they presuppose a close network of relationships in the faith community which is foreign to our individualistic, Sunday-go-to-meeting Western Christianity. Peter's words, familiar as they are, evoke a strange and elusive pattern of living together which nonetheless befits the members of God's household

The phrase 'one another' (which is one word in the Greek: *allelous*, 4:9) 'rings out like a peal of bells in the New Testament'.[86]

To love … prefer … edify … welcome … admonish … care for … comfort … encourage one another, Peter adds *'offer hospitality to one another'*.

Hospitality was a crucial act of love in the first century especially in meeting the needs of travelling Christians in an inhospitable society where inns were unreliable and unsafe (cf 3 John 5–8).[87]

Surely, too, there is a wider application beyond the circle of the Church. In our own alienation and rootlessness we have been welcomed home by the love of God-in-Trinity. In which case, as Henri Nouwen puts it, 'Hospitality … means primarily the creation of a free space where the stranger can enter and become a friend instead of an enemy. Hospitality is not to change people but to offer them space where change can take place.'[88]

In welcoming strangers we may, perchance, entertain angels unawares (Heb. 13:1–2)!

The wonderful story of the French Protestant village of Le Chambon is often cited as a glorious episode in the lean history of hospitality.

Led by their local pastor, André Trocmé, Le Chambon – a village of about 3,000 people – sheltered and saved a large number of Jews during the Nazi occupation of France. Philip Hallie, who made their story famous, later revisited the village to try to understand their actions. 'I learned that the opposite of cruelty is not simply freedom from the cruel relationships; it is *hospitality*.'

When he asked the villagers why they had done what they did, they replied 'What else could we do?' and seemed amused and embarrassed that he thought them especially good people.[89]

What else should Christians do?

Later, when Hallie visited America to tell the tale, a Jewish woman stood in a public meeting and said that the villagers had saved three of her children. Stepping to the podium, she told Hallie's audience, 'The Holocaust was storm, lightning, thunder, wind, rain ... yes. And Le Chambon was the rainbow.'[90]

Hospitality to the endangered is the rainbow of living hope above a sin-drenched world, hinting that the sun is breaking through the all-enveloping gloom.

Hospitality is just one of the *charismatic gifts* of which all Christians are stewards (4:10–11).

The 'charismata' are God's grace-gifts to equip His household. And Peter is as keenly interested as Paul in their proper exercise:

- 'Each one' is graced with some gift for the sake of the whole house; no one is excluded.
- What we have is only what we have received, so the grace-gifts should evoke humility, not pride.
- Everything we do and say is to be placed at the service of the community.
- All that we receive of God's grace we receive on trust for others and it is therefore to be 'faithfully administered' in their interests.
- To offer hospitality, or to exercise any other of the full range of spiritual gifts, is to perform, in Brett Webb-Mitchell's telling phrase, the *'Christly gestures'* which serve the Church,

ministering to it as God's household of grace, and making it credible to outsiders.[91]

God's household is lavishly provided for by God Himself.

- In *gifts* that exhibit the 'various forms' of God's multicoloured grace (4:10). The word found here is *poikiles*, used in the Septuagint of Joseph's coat of many colours!
- In *words* (4:11a) that convey the very utterance of God Himself – a solemn responsibility not to be taken lightly or reduced to glib speech.
- In *actions* (4:11b) that demonstrate a power beyond our powers, the very outgoing love of God. The word found here – *choregeo* – is of interest because it is a theatrical word used for an impresario's supply of resources that makes a drama happen. It is also worth saying that God's empowerment does not *always* bypass our natural strengths but refines and enhances them.

Since it is God's multi-faceted generosity, God's effective words, and God's energies that make His household work, all that we do and say tends to *His glory* (4:11c–12).

If we love and welcome and speak and serve in this way then 'God's bright presence will be evident in everything through Jesus, and *he'll* get all the credit as the One mighty in everything – encores to the end of time. Oh yes!' (4:11, *The Message*).

4:12–19 Suffering for glory

Suffering for Being a Christian

[12]Dear friends, do not be surprised at the painful trial you are suffering, as though something strange were happening to you. [13]But rejoice that you participate in the sufferings of Christ, so that you may be overjoyed when his glory is revealed. [14]If you are

insulted because of the name of Christ, you are blessed, for the Spirit of glory and of God rests on you. [15]If you suffer, it should not be as a murderer or thief or any other kind of criminal, or even as a meddler. [16]However, if you suffer as a Christian, do not be ashamed, but praise God that you bear that name. [17]For it is time for judgment to begin with the family of God; and if it begins with us, what will the outcome be for those who do not obey the gospel of God? [18]And,

> 'If it is hard for the righteous to be saved,
>> what will become of the ungodly and the sinner?'

[19]So then, those who suffer according to God's will should commit themselves to their faithful Creator and continue to do good.

Passages like this are embarrassingly foreign to comfortable Western Christians like myself. God's people – emblazoned with God's honorific titles as they are – are nevertheless, here and always, a cruciform people. We must 'reckon with the fact', Douglas John Hall reminds us, 'that there is more in the New Testament about the suffering of the church than about any other single theme or issue of ecclesiology'.[92]

God's people, who are being shaped into Christlike differentness, may not expect always to be popular. Jesus warned as much (Matt. 5:10–11).

In Douglas John Hall's words, Christian discipleship is 'a quest for and witness to truth in the midst of societies that lie, for authentic goodness in the midst of societies that reward duplicity, for true beauty in the midst of societies that celebrate kitsch and sentimentality.'[93]

As this is the case we can *expect to encounter hostility and opposition* (4:12). Peter's realism is refreshing: 'do not be surprised…', 'don't think it strange…' The strangeness comes with the territory. Not everyone liked Jesus! Why should we assume everyone will like us? From the 'Alpha' start of our

Christian lives we do well to recognise that the road ahead, which follows in His footsteps (2:21ff.), is no primrose path, no easy road, and is lined with crosses.

How, then, might Christians make sense of opposition and any suffering that ensues? By seeing such experiences as *'trials' or testing* (4:12). As in 1:7 they can refine our faith and test its genuineness.

In experiencing such trials we *share the identity and destiny of Jesus* (4:13). We may even rejoice to share the cruciform pattern of His life for the sake of sharing also in His glory when it is fully revealed.

We are sustained in these trials by our *perspective on the future* (4:13c). We dare to live differently because we have a sense of the big story – of the eschaton and of future glory (cf 4:7).

In the late seventeenth century a young Huguenot girl named Mary Durant was urged by the authorities to repudiate the Protestant 'heresy'. When she refused to recant she was thrown into a tower with thirty other women and incarcerated for thirty-eight years! She and the other women scratched on the walls of their prison the word *resistez*, still to be seen to this day.

Karl Olsen, who tells her story, wonders at the resistance of a young woman as time withers her and her prospects, and she passes into middle and old age. Struggling to come to terms with such steadfastness, Olsen's verdict leaps off the page: 'We cannot understand a faith which is not nourished by the temporal hope that tomorrow things will get better.'[94]

Christians are *provided with supernatural resources* (4:14). This is a wonderful truth. The Spirit is the Spirit of glory and He rests upon those who are suffering. No wonder the martyrs are radiant at the last!

Exposed to shame and disgrace, the suffering Christian is clothed in the vestments of honour by the very Spirit of God's glory. Cursed, he has blessing bestowed upon him by the Spirit!

Christians *have something worth suffering for – the name of*

Christ (4:15–16). This is suffering in the noblest cause. It is said that the psychology of suicide bombers is to 're-identify themselves by dying'. But, of course, it is a dying that kills and maims others. Not so the suffering Church; like its Master, it lays down its life for others because it already has an assured identity in Christ.

The suffering Church *anticipates the judgment of God* (4:17–19). Is the suggestion that martyrdoms purify the Church? Whatever the point of the Church's pain in the grand scheme of things, God is proved in it to be faithful and to be good (4:19). These are the rock-solid convictions of the apostles and of all believers which may enable them to view trials as opportunities for faith.

We can safely follow God's Son and do God's will knowing that He will not let us down, that He does not lead us into futile ways, and that He will do us only good now and at the last.

Prayer and Reflection

Lord, we thank You for giving us a different and longer view of
    Your future.
Lord, such vision enables us to think straight and not to
    squander our gifts in short-term living.
Lord, we thank You for blessing us with enough love to make
    ends meet:
        Jew and Gentile,
        rich and poor,
        black and white,
meeting and breaking bread at one table,
enjoying together Christ's hospitality.

Lord, You give us a high calling as
   trustees of Your future,
   stewards of Your grace-gifts,
   speaking God-given words
   serving in God-given strength.

And should we be called to suffer, why should we be surprised,
for 'Did not the Christ have to suffer to enter into His glory?'

And if we are insulted for being Your disciples – as well we may
be – surprise us with blessing, for does not 'the Spirit of glory
and of God rest' on those who bear the name?

Fair Judge, who starts with us Your own people,
Faithful Creator God, whose final word is grace,
We trust our very lives to You again.
Amen.

- With others, think about the details of your lives as believers
  and seek to rediscover those small but 'Christly gestures'
  which, if practised, might make a difference.
- How well does the prospect of 'the end' motivate us and help
  us keep things in true perspective?

1 PETER

5:1-9 Stooping in grace to conquer

To Elders and Young Men

[1]To the elders among you, I appeal as a fellow elder, a witness of Christ's sufferings and one who also will share in the glory to be revealed: [2]Be shepherds of God's flock that is under your care, serving as overseers – not because you must, but because you are willing, as God wants you to be; not greedy for money, but eager to serve; [3]not lording it over those entrusted to you, but being examples to the flock. [4]And when the Chief Shepherd appears, you will receive the crown of glory that will never fade away.

[5]Young men, in the same way be submissive to those who are older. All of you, clothe yourselves with humility towards one another, because,

'God opposes the proud
but gives grace to the humble.'

[6]Humble yourselves, therefore, under God's mighty hand, that he may lift you up in due time. [7]Cast all your anxiety on him because he cares for you.

[8]Be self-controlled and alert. Your enemy the devil prowls around like a roaring lion looking for someone to devour. [9]Resist him, standing firm in the faith, because you know that your brothers throughout the world are undergoing the same kind of sufferings.

I cannot read this section of the letter without hearing in it Peter's autobiography. Peter learned humility the hard way. Humility now becomes the resting-place of a wiser man with nothing more to lose.

5:1 Peter writes as a *fellow elder*

He appeals to the leaders of the churches in Asia Minor who will be responsible for reading the letter aloud to the people.

'Fellow elder'? That was far from Peter's original style. He once wanted to be the braveheart of the pack. 'Even if they all betray You, I won't!' he promised (Mark 14:29). How easily the proud ambition had clouded his judgment. Then, after tasting the bitterness of failure and defeat, he hears the Voice wryly probing his discomfort: 'Do you truly love me *more* than these?' (John 21:15). Now, tempered by truth and experience, Peter is content to be a 'fellow elder'.

5:1 Peter writes as an *eye witness of the sufferings of Christ*

Nothing can ever deny Peter the right to say, 'I was there.' It roots his apostleship in personally verifiable testimony.

Peter relishes the unique standpoint he enjoyed. The way he talks of loving Jesus speaks of personal acquaintance and intimacy. His description of the meekness and sufferings of the Master reads vividly like a first-hand account. Already he has learned from the risen Lord Himself (cf Luke 24:27ff.), and by his own failure and restoration, that the path to glory passes through suffering and humiliation. Already a sharer in the one, he confidently expects to share the other. Whatever your current sufferings, he assures his readers, they are offset by the coming glory.

5:2–4 Peter writes as an *under-shepherd of God's flock*

What bitter-sweet memories such language evokes for Peter. With the scars of his threefold denial graciously, tenderly probed by the threefold question 'Do you love me?', Peter is restored and charged with the task of feeding Christ's sheep and lambs.

Peter had followed the Good Shepherd and watched Him lay down His life for the sheep (John 10:11,15). He had met the Great Shepherd of the sheep after His resurrection (cf Heb.13:20). Now he urges his fellow leaders faithfully to serve the Chief Shepherd not because they are compelled to but because they want to; not for gain but freely and willingly; not by seeking to lord it over the flock but by behaving like the Lord of the flock and earning the right to lead by their example.

In a society ragingly competetive as regards status and honour, Peter was content to commend to all the under-shepherds the waiting crown of glory as the Master Shepherd's accolade.

5:5 Peter writes as one who *knows how hard humility is for the young especially!*

Jesus' final word to Peter was a heart-stopping prophetic warning. Young men – as Peter knew only too well – are headstrong and self-determined. So Peter had blustered and blundered his way through 'to bring the kingdom in' and resisted any talk of crosses! But when you are old, Jesus had told him, you will, paradoxically, become childlike again because you will stretch out your hands and others will clothe you and lead you where you do not want to go (John 21:18). But then the cockcrow which once signalled denial may herald the dawning of a new day.

5:5b–7 Peter writes as one who knows that *'God opposes the proud but gives grace to the humble'* who receive it with open hands

'Clothe yourselves with humility.' 'Put on the apron of humility ...' Peter could surely not have written that without the memories flooding back of that unforgettable evening when the Master Himself took a towel and the basin and stooped to wash their dirty feet (John 13:1–17). The One to whom the most was given bending to serve the least.

But is not humbling yourself like this a risk? Might I not be crushed under such a mighty hand? Perhaps it would be better fearfully to preserve my life, protect my anxious self-interest and keep my options open! Then what will I do with the mountain of anxiety I carry?

The alternative is to bow low under His hand of grace and be lifted up to look in His face, seeing in His eyes the love to take my anxiety from me, if I let Him.

5:8-9a Peter writes to *warn of the devil's dangers*

Who better than Peter to tell us about this! The devil prowls around but is not irresistible. You can resist him, firm in your faith.

Peter's warning is born of deep personal experience. It was satanic talk he had once blurted out when seeking to forestall the way of the cross (Matt. 16:23).

A servant girl by an open fire had shattered his boldness and made him disown his Lord. Satan had indeed sifted him like wheat. But, Peter rejoices, Jesus had prayed for him that his faith would not utterly fail (Luke 22:31–32). And so it proved. Here Peter is, putting the devil in his place, as Jesus has done.

5:9 Peter writes *in solidarity with suffering Christians throughout the known world*

Be stirred, he urges us, by the courage shown by the worldwide community of faith. So the modern Western Christian acknowledges with awe and thankfulness the brave witness of the martyred Church today. 'Millions of Christians around the world do in fact live in constant danger of persecution or forced conversion, from either governments or local vigilantes.'[95]

Peter's words ring true for countless Christians in Nigeria, Egypt, the Sudan, Pakistan, Indonesia and in many other places. From them we can take heart in our local and often lesser pressures.

5:10–11 Strengthened by grace for glory

[10]And the God of all grace, who called you to his eternal glory in Christ, after you have suffered a little while, will himself restore you and make you strong, firm and steadfast. [11]To him be the power for ever and ever. Amen.

God is characteristically the 'God of all grace', demonstrating a generosity and lavishness that sponsors every aspect of our salvation from start to finish.

The prophets anticipated the grace of salvation that was to come to us and that has been established among us by Christ and in us by the Spirit (1:10). For his part, Peter urges us to look forward to the grace of salvation that is yet to come to us when Christ returns (1:13).

In typical Greco-Roman letter form, 1 Peter, in keeping with most New Testament epistles, begins with the customary greetings: 'Grace and peace be yours' (1:2c).

Again in typical Greco-Roman cultural style, God is regarded as the Supreme Patron and Benefactor. God's grace is classically viewed as God's undeserved favour towards us.

But this is only part of the story. As David de Silva observes, what is distinctive about God's grace is not that it is bestowed freely and without coercion. Every benefactor did this, even, according to the writer Seneca, to the ungrateful – though only if the patron had resources left over after benefiting the virtuous! What is unique about God's grace poured out in Christ is that it is bestowed not out of His surplus but out of His fullness, and not only on the ungrateful but on His enemies who are caught in active rebellion and hostility towards Him![96]

God's grace is an active energy, the outgoing of divine love and mercy, concentrated in Christ and focused especially in His self-giving on the cross which reconciles us to God. As we look in faith to the Christ who died for us, God's favour and forgiveness flow to us.

Grace is the outgoing energy of God that sustains and provides resources for Christians at every turn. By it marriage is sweetened and strengthened (3:7). Every charismatic gift which builds up the Church is a grace-gift that redounds to the glory of God (4:10). Grace is the strength that nourishes and supplies the Church.

Grace comes to us on its own terms, not ours. Grace comes as a gift to our poverty, not a triumph of our resources. We come to receive grace with empty hands. God resists those who are self-sufficient, independent, and proud, but 'gives grace to the humble' (5:5).

The God of all grace will 'restore' us, for grace is the great healer of our wounds, mending our broken lives, repairing the damage we incur in serving Him.

The God of all grace will 'strengthen' us as He did Peter himself (Luke 22:32).

The God of all grace will 'establish' you and 'make you firm and steadfast', for God is the Master Builder and grace the sure foundation of our lives.

And 'after you have suffered a little while', in the words of John Newton's hymn, ''tis grace will lead [us] home'.

This is the 'true grace' of God (5:12) – real, authentic, totally reliable and supportive even through suffering.

It was the soon-to-be martyred Dietrich Bonhoeffer who, out of the shadow of Nazi oppression, warned us against devaluing God's grace. 'Cheap grace is forgiveness without repentance, grace without discipleship, grace without the cross, grace without Jesus Christ, living and incarnate.' Costly grace, on the other hand, said Bonhoeffer, is 'the treasure hidden in the field; for the sake of it a man will gladly go and sell all that he has'. Such grace 'is costly because it costs a man his life ... and above all, because it cost God the life of his Son'.[97]

It is this costly grace that lays claim to our wholehearted response. Grace initiates the process by calling us to follow Christ, and grace sustains us in the courage to walk in His footsteps all the way to the final vindication He has secured for us.

We may be confident, then, with John Newton: ''Tis grace has brought me safe thus far, and grace will lead me home' to the eternal glory (cf 1:7; 1:11 where according to the Christ-pattern glory lies beyond suffering; 4:11; 4:13 His glory; 4:14 the Spirit of glory transfigures in the midst of suffering; 5:4 the crown of glory).

This is our destiny under grace. We agree with Philip Doddridge:

Grace taught my soul to pray,
and pardoning love to know;
'Twas grace that kept me to this day,
and will not let me go.

In Jane Crewdson's words:

And He who is Himself the Gift and Giver,
the future glory and the present smile,
with the bright promise of the glad forever,
will light the shadows of the 'little while'.

5:12–14 Standing firm in true grace

Final Greetings
[12]With the help of Silas, whom I regard as a faithful brother, I have written to you briefly, encouraging you and testifying that this is the true grace of God. Stand fast in it. [13]She who is in Babylon, chosen together with you, sends you her greetings, and so does my son Mark. [14]Greet one another with a kiss of love. Peace to all of you who are in Christ.

Peter writes *from Rome*. Babylon was the place of exile for the Jews then swallowed up by the Babylonians. Almost certainly 'Babylon' is a cryptic name for Rome. It may therefore stand symbolically for any world power or organised system in opposition to God – the prevailing 'imperial' order under which 'she', that is, God's local people, lives (5:12).

Peter, in effect, is connecting with his readers as he has described them in 1:1 and is speaking as a fellow exile from his own 'Babylon'.

Peter, the once rugged individualist, is now pleased to acknowledge others in the faith. Peter, the once lone ranger, now needs Silas as his amanuensis. As far as we can tell, Silas – or Silvanus to give him his Latin name – was a well-to-do Jew with a good literary and rhetorical education. As Peter dictated to him, Silas no doubt tweaked his grammar and smoothed his prose. In this microcosm of the 'Church', the big fisherman relies on his learned secretary and enjoys the company of Mark.

The gesture which Peter so bitterly remembered as the kiss of betrayal is now enacted as the kiss of covenant love.

Peter offers true grace and calls for true grit without illusions but with living hope.

Peter writes from the heart of the empire to the hearts of the exiles. And his final word is 'peace'.

Prayer and Reflection

Lord, thank You for the apostle Peter,
For all he became because You believed in him and prayed
for him.
For all the ways in which we hear Your voice through the
vividness and the truthfulness of his testimony, we give You
thanks.

As Peter exhorts us,
    we humble ourselves that grace may lift us up,
    we offload our weight of worry onto You that grace may
    bear the burden for us,
    we resist the evil one that grace may nerve us for battle and
    see us through the fight.

Especially we identify with all our fellow Christians throughout
the world who are suffering for their faith.
In solidarity with them, we plead Your special tough grace for
the persecuted Church in
    Sudan
    Burma
    Indonesia
    Nigeria
    Pakistan
    Egypt ...
May Your living Church continue to be the anvil that wears
out many hammers.

O God of all-restoring grace, make us strong in Peter's apostolic
faith, and keep us firmly on track for Your eternal glory.
Amen.

- Reflect on how Peter's own story as a disciple and apostle of Jesus is reflected in this letter and how we might take heart from it.
- Check out the work of Christian Solidarity Worldwide (CSW): in the UK (http://www.cws.org.uk); in the USA (http://www.cswusa.com); in Australia (email: cswoz@hotmail.com); in Hong Kong (http://www.csw.org.hk). Weave your findings into intercessory prayers in your group and in your church for suffering Christians around the world.

Resources

Commentaries on 1 Peter

Scot McKnight, *1 Peter: The NIV Application Commentary* (Grand Rapids: Zondervan, 1996). Another fine example of this increasingly useful series. Bang up to date and by reputable evangelical scholars. Accessible to the general reader.

J. Ramsey Michaels, *1 Peter: Word Biblical Commentary* (Waco: Word Books, 1988). Thorough and detailed and rich in comment for the more technically-minded reader.

I. Howard Marshall, *1 Peter: The IVP New Testament Commentaries* (Leicester: IVP, 1991). Very useful shorter commentary by one of the leading evangelical scholars in the UK.

Special studies

John H. Elliott, *A Home for the Homeless: A Sociological Exegesis of 1 Peter, Its Situation and Strategy* (London: SCM Press, 1981). A ground-breaking and much debated work that opens windows on the social situation of Peter's readers.

David de Silva, *Honor, Patronage, Kinship & Purity: Unlocking New Testament Culture* (Downers Grove: IVP, 2000). I am much indebted to this brilliant and fascinating book.

'Tracts for the times'

William Willimon and Stanley Hauerwas, *Resident Aliens, Life in the Christian Colony* (Nashville: Abingdon Press, 1989). Superb, provocative bestseller from two of the Church's sharpest minds.

See also their *Where Resident Aliens Live: Exercises for Christian Practice* (Nashville: Abingdon Press, 1996).

Notes

1. The first possibility is endorsed by J.H. Elliott; the second stance is cautiously adopted by most conservative commentators including the most recent, J. Ramsey Michaels and Scot McKnight. Both viewpoints are in sharp distinction from more critical scholarship which wants to place 1 Peter at the end of the first century.

2. Luke T. Johnson, *The Writings of the New Testament: An Interpretation* (London: SCM Press, 1986), p.435.

3. Scot McKnight, *1Peter: The NIV Application Commentary* (Grand Rapids: Zondervan, 1996), p.26. McKnight is interacting with the research of J.H. Elliott, *A Home for the Homeless: A Sociological Exegesis of 1 Peter, Its Situation and Strategy* (London: SCM Press), 1982.

4. Ibid., p.51.

5. On this theme of journey see J. Ramsey Michaels, 'Going to Heaven with Jesus: From 1 Peter to Pilgrim's Progress' in ed. Richard N. Longenecker, *Patterns of Discipleship in the New Testament* (Grand Rapids: Eerdmans, 1996), pp.248–268.

6. Elliott, op cit., p.132.

7. Ibid, p.132.

8. David de Silva, *Honor, Patronage, Kinship and Purity: Unlocking the New Testament* (Downers Grove: IVP, 2000), p.73.

9. Ibid., p.43.

10. Ibid., p.47.

11. Ibid., p.45.

12. Ibid., p.43.

13. Alain de Botton, *Status Anxiety* (London: Hamish Hamilton, 2004), pp.115–117.

14. Ibid., p.261.

15. Ibid., p.53.

16. J. Ramsey Michaels, '1 Peter' in ed. Ralph Martin and Peter H. Davids, *Dictionary of the Later New Testament and Its Development* (Downers Grove: IVP, 1997), p.920.

17. Richard Bauckham, 'James, 1 Peter, Jude, and 2 Peter' in ed. Marcus Bockmuehl and Michael B. Thompason, *A Vision For the Church: Studies in Early Christian Ecclesiology in Honour of J.P.M. Sweet* (Edinburgh: T & T Clark, 1997), p.160. I am indebted to Bauckham in this whole section.

18. Ibid., p.163.

19. Jonathan R. Wilson, *Gospel Virtues: Practising Faith, Hope and Love in*

Uncertain Times (Downers Grove: IVP, 1998), p.43.

20. Stanley Hauerwas, *The Peaceable Kingdom* (London: SCM Press, 1984), p.100.

21. Colin Gunton, *The Christian Faith* (Oxford: Blackwell's, 2002), p.188.

22. Peter Kreeft, *Fundamentals of the Faith: Essays in Christian Apologetics* (San Francisco: Ignatius Press, 1988), p.177.

23. Ibid., p.177.

24. Mark Buchanan, *Your God is Too Safe* (Oregon: Multnomah, 2001), p.65.

25. Lewis Smedes, *Standing on the Promises: Keeping Hope Alive For a Tomorrow We Cannot Control* (Nashville: Thomas Nelson, 1998), pp.153–154.

26. A.W. Tozer, *Who Put Jesus On The Cross?* (Camp Hill: Christian Publications, 1975), p.149.

27. Ray Palmer, 'Jesus, these eyes have never seen', Baptist Hymn Book, no. 206.

28. Larry W. Hurtado, *Lord Jesus Christ: Devotion To Jesus in Earliest Christianity* (Grand Rapids: Eerdmans, 2003), p.2.

29. Ibid., p.653.

30. Wayne A. Grudem, *The First Epistle of Peter* (Leicester: Inter-Varsity, 1988), p.73.

31. Jürgen Moltmann, *Experiences of God* (London: SCM Press, 1980), p.33.

32. Wilson, op.cit. p.99. There is much wisdom packed into this small book. Wilson goes on to add, 'Hope finds its identity in the living tradition of the gospel, and is determined by the particular *telos* – the eschaton of the gospel.' (p.99).

33. John Webster, *Holiness* (London: SCM Press, 2003), p.46. Webster's whole discussion is very illuminating.

34. J.C. Ryle, *Holiness* (reprinted, Wilmington: AP & A Publishers, nd.), p.22.

35. J.I. Packer, *A Passion for Holiness* (Cambridge: Crossway, 1992), p.9.

36. Ryle, op.cit., p.24.

37. Stanley Hauerwas, *Sanctify Them in Truth: Holiness Exemplified* (Edinburgh: T & T Clark, 1998), pp.197–198.

38. Webster, op.cit., p.94.

39. Ibid., pp.92–93.

40. Paul S. Minear, *The Bible and the Historian: Breaking the Silence about God in Biblical Studies* (Nashville: Abingdon, 2002), p.192.

41. Webster, op.cit., p.96.

42. Ibid., p.73.

43. E.G. Selwyn, *The First Epistle of Peter* (London: Macmillan, 1961), p.158.

44. J. Ramsey Michaels, *1 Peter: Word Biblical Commentary* (Waco: Word Books, 1988), p.98.

45. John V. Taylor, *The Go-Between God: The Holy Spirit and the Christian Mission* (London: SCM Press, 1972), p.5.

46. Samuel Chadwick, *The Way to Pentecost* (London: Hodder & Stoughton, 1932), p.15.

47. See the helpful note by David de Silva in op.cit., p.54, n.22.

48. P.T. Forsyth, *Rome, Reaction and Reform* (London: Hodder & Stoughton, 1899), p.213.

49. For a helpful discussion of holiness as

differentness see David Gill's superb little book, *Becoming Good: Building Moral Character* (Downers Grove: IVP, 2000), pp.113–123.

50. Webster, op.cit., p.58.

51. Philip Greenslade, *A Passion for God's Story* (Carlisle: Paternoster Press, 2002), p.98.

52. Gerhard Lohfink, *Does God Need the Church? Towards a Theology of the People of God* (Collegeville: The Liturgical Press, 1999), p.38.

53. William J.Abraham, 'I Believe in One Holy, Catholic, and Apostolic Church' in ed. Christopher R. Seitz, *Nicene Christianity: The Future for a New Ecumenism* (Grand Rapids: Brazos Press, 2001), pp.186–187.

54. Norman Kraus, *The Community of the Spirit: How the Church is in the World* (Scottdale: Herald Press, 1993), p.120.

55. Karl Barth, *Call for God* (London: SCM Press, 1967), pp.24–25.

56. Robert Wilkin, *The Christians as the Romans Saw Them* (New Haven: Yale University Press, 1984), p.63.

57. Judith Gundry-Volf and Miroslav Volf, *A Spacious Heart: Essays on Identity and Belonging* (Harrisburg:Trinity International, 1997), p.43.

58. Elliott, op.cit., p.35.

59. J.R.R. Tolkein, *The Lord of the Rings* (London: Harper-Collins, 1991), p.87.

60. David de Silva offers this closer reading of the text in op.cit., p.144, n.49.

61. Martin Hengel offers the widest coverage in *The Cross of the Son of God* (London: SCM Press, 1986), pp.93–185.

62. James Denney, *The Death of Christ* (London: Hodder, 1911), p.67.

63. Martin Hengel, *The Charismatic Leader and His Followers* (Edinburgh: T & T Clark, 1981), p.72.

64. T.S. Eliot 'East Coker' in *Four Quartets* (London: Faber and Faber, 1959), p.29.

65. Peter Kreeft, *Making Sense of Suffering* (London: Hodder & Stoughton, 1986), p.139.

66. Jürgen Moltmann, *The Crucified God* (London: SCM Press, 1974), p.7.

67. As recalled by John Randolph Taylor, *God Loves Like That: The Theology of James Denney* (London: SCM Press, 1962), p.79.

68. Margaret Attwood, *The Handmaid's Tale* (London: Vintage, 1996), p.34.

69. G.K. Chesterton, 'Ballad of the White Horse' in *The Collected Poems of G.K. Chesterton* (London: Methuen, 1942), p.257. Chesterton's comment, of course, has the horse particularly in mind.

70. Despite the valiant attempts of many commentators, I doubt that the issue can be softened by appeal to Eph. 5:21 in support of alleged 'mutual submission' – an idea contradicted by the 'case studies' which immediately follow in which the relationships are never reversed, ie, husbands are never said to be subject to wives nor parents to children.

71. Allen Verhey, *Remembering Jesus: Christian Community, Scripture and the Moral Life* (Grand Rapids: Eerdmans, 2002). Verhey's discussion of the topic and interaction with Margaret Attwood's novel has greatly stimulated my thinking.

72. Bruce W. Winter, *Roman Wives, Roman Widows: The Appearance of New Women and the Pauline Communities* (Grand Rapids: Eerdmans, 2003), pp.4–5.

73. Ibid., p.122.

74. For a popular discussion of this whole matter see further Mike Starkey, *Fashion and Style* (Crowborough: Monarch, 1995).

75. Grudem, op.cit., p.143.

76. Smedes, op.cit., p.90.

77. Verhey, op.cit., pp.210–211.

78. Richard Morris, *Cheshire; The Biography of Leonard Cheshire, VC, OM* (London: Viking, 2000), p.373.

79. Denney, op.cit., p.73.

80. Ramsey Michaels, *1 Peter*, op.cit., p.205.

81. Peter Davids, *The First Epistle of Peter: The New International Commentary on the New Testament* (Grand Rapids: Eerdmans, 1990), p.137.

82. Howard Marshall, *1 Peter: The IVP New Testament Commentaries* (Leicester: IVP, 1991), pp.123ff.

83. The standard work on baptism in the New Testament is by my revered teacher, George Beasley-Murray, *Baptism in the New Testament* (London: Macmillan, 1963), to which, among much else, I am deeply indebted.

84. Ibid., p.261.

85. Ibid., p.262.

86. John V. Taylor, op.cit., p.126. On the 'one anothers' see the fine study by Gerald Sittser, *Loving Across the Differences* (Downers Grove: IVP, 1994).

87. See on this Elliott, op.cit., pp.145–148.

88. Henri Nouwen, *Reaching Out* (Glasgow: Collins, 1980), pp.68–69. See also Wilson, op.cit., chapter 8, and the essays by Christine Pohl, Gilbert Bond and Reinhard Hutter in eds. Miroslav Volf and Dorothy Bass, *Practising Theology: Beliefs and Practices in Christian Life* (Grand Rapids: Eerdmans, 2002).

89. As quoted by Wilson, op.cit., p.177.

90. The story is told by Smedes, op.cit., pp.145–146, and also by Os Guinness, *Long Journey Home* (Grand Rapids: Zondervan, 2001), pp. 152–154.

91. Brett Webb-Mitchell, *Christly Gestures: Learning to Be Members of the Body of Christ* (Grand Rapids: Eerdmans, 2003).

92. Douglas John Hall, *The Cross in Our Context: Jesus and the Suffering World* (Minneapolis: Fortress Press, 2003), p.138.

93. Ibid., p.142.

94. The story is told by John Piper in *The Purifying Power of Living by Faith in Future Grace* (Leicester: IVP, 1995, pp.171–172). Piper cites Karl Olsen's book, *Passion* (New York: Harper and Row, 1963), pp.116–117, and reflects movingly on the story.

95. Philip Jenkins, *The Next Christendom: The Coming of Global Christianity* (Oxford: Oxford University Press, 2002), p.218.

96. de Silva, op.cit., p.129.

97. Dietrich Bonhoeffer, *The Cost of Discipleship* (London: SCM Press, 1959), pp.36–37.

National Distributors

UK: (and countries not listed below)
CWR, Waverley Abbey House, Waverley Lane, Farnham, Surrey GU9 8EP.
Tel: (01252) 784700 Outside UK +44 1252 784700

AUSTRALIA: CMC Australasia, PO Box 519, Belmont, Victoria 3216.
Tel: (03) 5241 3288

CANADA: Cook Communications Ministries, PO Box 98, 55 Woodslee Avenue, Paris, Ontario.
Tel: 1800 263 2664

GHANA: Challenge Enterprises of Ghana, PO Box 5723, Accra.
Tel: (021) 222437/223249 Fax: (021) 226227

HONG KONG: Cross Communications Ltd, 1/F, 562A Nathan Road, Kowloon.
Tel: 2780 1188 Fax: 2770 6229

INDIA: Crystal Communications, 10-3-18/4/1, East Marredpalli, Secunderabad – 500026,
Andhra Pradesh.
Tel/Fax: (040) 27737145

KENYA: Keswick Books and Gifts Ltd, PO Box 10242, Nairobi.
Tel: (02) 331692/226047 Fax: (02) 728557

MALAYSIA: Salvation Book Centre (M) Sdn Bhd, 23 Jalan SS 2/64, 47300 Petaling Jaya, Selangor.
Tel: (03) 78766411/78766797 Fax: (03) 78757066/78756360

NEW ZEALAND: CMC Australasia, PO Box 36015, Lower Hutt.
Tel: 0800 449 408 Fax: 0800 449 049

NIGERIA: FBFM, Helen Baugh House, 96 St Finbarr's College Road, Akoka, Lagos.
Tel: (01) 7747429/4700218/825775/827264

PHILIPPINES: OMF Literature Inc, 776 Boni Avenue, Mandaluyong City.
Tel: (02) 531 2183 Fax: (02) 531 1960

SINGAPORE: Armour Publishing Pte Ltd, Block 203A Henderson Road,
11–06 Henderson Industrial Park, Singapore 159546.
Tel: 6 276 9976 Fax: 6 276 7564

SOUTH AFRICA: Struik Christian Books, 80 MacKenzie Street, PO Box 1144, Cape Town 8000.
Tel: (021) 462 4360 Fax: (021) 461 3612

SRI LANKA: Christombu Books, 27 Hospital Street, Colombo 1.
Tel: (01) 433142/328909

TANZANIA: CLC Christian Book Centre, PO Box 1384, Mkwepu Street, Dar es Salaam.
Tel/Fax (022) 2119439

ZIMBABWE: Word of Life Books, Shop 4, Memorial Building, 35 S Machel Avenue, Harare.
Tel: (04) 781305 Fax: (04) 774739

For email addresses, visit the CWR website: www.cwr.org.uk

CWR is a registered charity – number 294387

Day and Residential Courses
Counselling Training
Leadership Development
Biblical Study Courses
Regional Seminars
Ministry to Women
Daily Devotionals
Books and Videos
Conference Centre

Trusted all Over the World

CWR HAS GAINED A WORLDWIDE
reputation as a centre of excellence for
Bible-based training and resources. From
our headquarters at Waverley Abbey
House, Farnham, England, we have been
serving God's people for 40 years with a
vision to help apply God's Word to
everyday life and relationships. The daily
devotional *Every Day with Jesus* is read by
over three-quarters of a million people in
more than 150 countries, and our unique
courses in biblical studies and pastoral
care are respected all over the world.
Waverley Abbey House provides a
conference centre in a tranquil setting.

For free brochures on our seminars and
courses, conference facilities, or a
catalogue of CWR resources, please
contact us at the following address.
**CWR, Waverley Abbey House, Waverley
Lane, Farnham, Surrey GU9 8EP, UK**

Telephone: **+44 (0)1252 784700**
Email: **mail@cwr.org.uk**
Website: **www.cwr.org.uk**

CWR's Online
Bookstore

Christian resources for everyday life and relationships

Offering a complete listing
of all CWR's products, our
Online Bookstore includes:

Our latest releases

A bargain basement

Forthcoming titles

Personalised pages

**CWR'S ONLINE
BOOKSTORE**

www.cwrstore.org.uk

Cover to Cover Bible Discovery:
1 & 2 Thessalonians
The Coming that Completes the Story

As Christians we live out our lives in the light of God's future.
And that future is the coming of Jesus to complete the story.
This prospect inspires a tenacious hope, shaping the way we
behave, and gives significance to everything we do. This is the
note Paul strikes throughout these two stimulating letters,
written to a very young but amazingly vibrant community
of believers who quickly became a 'model' church.

£5.99
ISBN: 1-85345-305-6

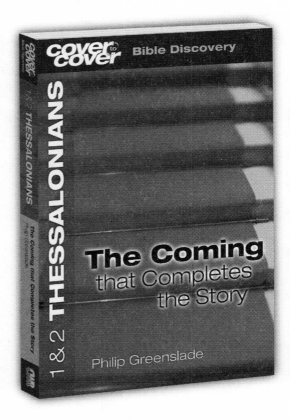

Cover to Cover Bible Discovery: Psalms
Songs for all Seasons

With thoughtful and inspiring insights, Philip Greenslade takes us on a journey of discovery to the heart of understanding the Bible. Using the framework of the four seasons, this book invites you to explore the world of the Psalms, the songbook of the Bible.

£7.99
ISBN: 1-85345-282-3

Cover to Cover Bible Discovery: Philippians
Rejoice! The King is Lord

In *Rejoice! The King is Lord* you are invited to discover afresh
the surpassing joy of knowing Jesus as Lord. The book sets
the challenge to the Church to be a 'colony of heaven' which
lives out a Christlike lifestyle.

£5.99

ISBN: 1-85345-281-5